The MemoryCare Plays

Edited by Margaret A. Noel

Cover Art: Harry Widman. *Three Shapes in Space.* **Ca 1984. Mixed media collage. 18 x 24 inches. Collection of Matthew Widman.**

Harry Widman (1929 -) is a noted Oregon artist and professor emeritus from the Pacific Northwest College of Art (formerly the Portland Museum Art School). Widman's artistic career spans seventy years and includes works in oil on canvas, mixed media collage, watercolor, ink, charcoal and wood sculpture. Primarily a painter in the New York abstract expressionist and modernist traditions, Widman's work utilizes color and form to create a visual language that draws from figurative imagery, the natural world, from poetry and from myth. Harry Widman was diagnosed with Alzheimer's disease in 2008.

Further inquiries and catalogue information at www.harrywidmanart.com

ISBN-13:
978-0615951188 (MemoryCare)

ISBN-10:
061595118X

Available from Amazon.com, CreateSpace.com, and other retail outlets.

These three extraordinary plays capture the pain and the joy, the confusion and the clarity, and the challenges and rewards of living with Alzheimer disease and caring for someone you love who has the illness. For those who do not know the illness they are a wonderful illustration of the ups and downs faced by those who do. By neither shying away from the difficulties nor glamorizing the humor and love that maintains patients and those supporting them, these playwrights capture the multiplicity of experiences and emotions of those living with Alzheimer disease.

> — Peter V. Rabins, MD, MPH, Professor of Psychiatry and Behavioral Sciences Johns Hopkins University School of Medicine, co-author, *The 36 Hour Day*

These three one-acts dramatize the emotional toll when the most complex grid in the human universe, the brain, malfunctions. They also show the value of genuine, loving care. They are simultaneously truthful, enriching, and moving.

> — Charles OyamO Gordon, Writer-in-Residence at The University of Michigan, author, *Boundless Grace* and *The Resurrection of Lady Lester*

This is universally accessible pure art offering rich, intimate, poignant and existentially complex moments in family life. You will find yourself being swept up in a kaleidoscope of time, the true essence of Alzheimer's disease. You will experience imperfect love, and subtlety leavened with humor, breaking down barriers between "us" and "them". Everything is here in the moment – the poignant, murky and hot-bottom authentic realities of living with memory disorders. You will care deeply for and about these believable individuals struggling to make sense of and maintain increasingly fragile connections. *The MemoryCare Plays* are fresh answers to increasing awareness and reducing stigma of individuals with dementia, and they accomplish this far more artfully than any advocacy messaging campaign to date.

> — Lisa P. Gwyther, MSW, LCSW, Director Duke Family Support Program, Durham (NC), co-author, *The Alzheimer's Action Plan*

The Memory Care Plays is a collection that marshals theater's unique power to confront the human condition with a gaze clear and unwavering, and ultimately all the more compassionate for being so.

> — Stuart Dybek, MacArthur Fellow and Whiting Writers' Award Winner, author, *The Coast of Chicago, I Sailed with Magellan*, and *Streets in Their Own Ink*

Although each is distinct, the three one-act plays presented here all reveal how Alzheimer's disease tears at the very fabric of families but at the same

time discover the deep resilience and humanity that is shared by the affected individual and their loved ones.
> — John C. Morris, MD, Friedman Distinguished Professor of Neurology and Director, Knight Alzheimer Disease Research Center, Washington University, St Louis

In the summer of 2013, I had the pleasure of reading the role of Tim in *Steering into the Skid.* For me, for the artist reading Amanda, and for the audience, the play was a brilliant stroke of lightning into a dark world. Each of the works in this moving anthology provides a unique look at the grief, the anger, and the love experienced by the victims—both the afflicted and the bystanders—of memory loss. For anyone touched by this unforgiving disease, and there are many of us, this rich volume is light in that dark.
> — Edward M. Moersfelder, Theatre Artist and Writer, St. Croix (WI) Festival Theatre

The MemoryCare Plays enhance our understanding of dementia through poignant illustrations of loss and love. Dr. Noel, a nationally recognized geriatrician, provides provocative discussion points for each play based on her experience caring for patients and families. A unique addition to the library of medical humanities, this work will influence physicians and physicians in training for years to come.
> — Marcia Wofford, MD, Associate Dean of Medical Education Wake Forest School of Medicine, Winston-Salem

These three, one-act plays succeed at entertaining us while raising our awareness of how the effects of dementia on a loved one changes family dynamics, especially for those who accept the challenge of providing daily care.
> — Ronald J. Manheimer, PhD, author, *A Map to the End of Time: Wayfaring with Friends and Philosophers*

Caregiving for a loved one with dementia is among life's greatest challenges and opportunities. These plays, which explore facets of the process, provide insights into the powerful impact caregiving has on the individuals and families involved. They are excellent resources and valuable tools for discussion and learning.
> — Carl Eisdorfer, MD, PhD, co-author, *Loss of Self* and of *Caring for Your Aging Parent*

MemoryCare has been recognized as an outstanding program for its compassionate and excellent care of patients and families. If you are caring for someone with dementia or know someone who is a caregiver, this anthology of plays will help you better understand the complexities that families face with this devastating disease.

— Dr. Murali Doraiswamy, Professor of Psychiatry and Medicine, Duke University, co-author, *The Alzheimer's Action Plan*

These three plays catch the light and shadow that play across the lives of people with dementia, and of our own along with theirs. Dr. Margaret Noel's playwriting competition was an inspired act of compassionate creation, and she deserves our deepest thanks: these plays get under our skin, when we might prefer the illusion of a cure that's right around the corner. We "steer into the skid" with Tim and Amanda as the intimacy of everyday forgetting shades imperceptibly into early Alzheimer's - and suddenly their private world is on display, made public by the act of diagnosis. We too are confused as Arthur comes untethered from the world of every day, but we ground ourselves again in his deep connection to those he loves if they can but join him in the beauty of the world he used to paint. And we ourselves enter into the watery ebb and flow of past and present that Isabel inhabits, so beautifully rendered in its unbounded time and its challenge to her children's own identity. These plays can help to make our communities more 'dementia-friendly', and they should be seen, or read at least, by everyone with a heart to make that happen.

— Soo Borson, MD, Professor (Emerita), University of Washington School of Medicine

Riding the Waves is creative, humorous, and deeply reflective of the nature of parent child relationships. I like the complexity and family dynamics of *In the Garden* and the reflection on the father's life as an artist. *Steering Into the Skid* is beautifully done. I love the spontaneous dialogue and the metaphor for time passing as Tim progresses through different stages.

— Tommy Hays, author, *The Pleasure Was Mine*

Memory is the glue that holds our mental lives together. Without the unifying force of memory our consciousness would be broken up into as many fragments as there are seconds in the day. Imagine a life without memory! In *The MemoryCare Plays* we see this illustrated brilliantly and empathically. These are wonderful plays that beautifully depict the tragedy of Alzheimer's for the patient and for the family.

— Eric Kandel, MD, University Professor, and Professor of Psychiatry Columbia University, recipient of the Nobel Prize in Physiology 2000

This book is dedicated to the brave ones who teach us to find meaning even as memory fades, and to all who spend themselves on the care of another.

CONTENTS

PREFACE

On the wall of my office is a framed cross-stitch of a quote by American playwright and novelist, Thornton Wilder, "Even memory is not necessary for love. There is a land of the living and a land of the dead, and the bridge is love, the only survival, the only meaning[1]." It gives me some modicum of peace, for in the best stories we hear in our clinic, this is true. Family narratives about dementia confront the tragedy of a unique type of loss. Our work calls us to prepare a family for a long, gradual fading of a person's ability to think, remember, communicate and act independently. What does it mean to protect, support, and love another human being through such an illness?

I had my own personal preparation for the job through the schooling of my grandmother's dementia. One would think a family might catch on when she appeared half-dressed on the hotel balcony at my brother's graduation. But that was 1977, I was a college student, and she was the wonderfully eccentric, fun and funny, devoted woman who single handedly gave me my great affection for "old people." Each year that followed multiplied the "eccentricities" until the final chapter 12 years later when all 74 pounds of her died in my arms. We never knew exactly what type of dementia she had, likely a combination of vascular dementia and Alzheimer's disease. Slowly losing her taught me that there had to be a better way of helping a family through this journey.

Twenty-five years have passed and I have the great fortune of being part of a better way. MemoryCare is a non-profit charitable organization in Asheville, North Carolina, that provides integrated medical and care management services for families affected by Alzheimer's disease and other dementias. Our mission is to provide specialized medical care to older adults with memory loss, to support caregivers with education, counseling, and improved access to services, and to provide community education. We simply do what needs to be done. Since 2000, when I founded MemoryCare, the

---

[1] Wilder, T. (2009). *The Bridge of San Luis Rey and Other Novels, 1926-1948.* (p. 107) New York: Library of America.

i

scientific evidence has mounted that effective dementia care requires educating and supporting the caregivers who show up for the job. Unfortunately, our current health care system has not yet been designed to incorporate caregivers. MemoryCare's first creative act was to find its support through a blended model of cost-sharing and community support. Through the generosity of many, we have survived and managed to care for thousands of patients and their families who are impacted by the progressive dependency, cognitive and personality changes of a loved one diagnosed with Alzheimer's disease or other types of dementia.

In the spring of 2012, as part of our mission to educate our community and to raise funds to care for our caregivers, MemoryCare put forth a call for one act plays that highlight the issues families face when a loved one suffers from dementia. We sought one act plays that dramatized the full complexity and richness of the caregiving relationship, including its challenges as well as its rewards. One of the most important things we do at MemoryCare is to help our patients and their caregivers tell their stories. These stories will help all other members of the family, professional caregivers, and other health care providers to remember who this person is, how they and their family function and most importantly, what they need to live life as fully as possible in the face of a difficult, heartbreaking illness.

In response to our call for original, never before produced one-act plays, we received 91 submissions from 24 states, Canada, England and Australia. After an initial screening by a panel of caregivers, a juried committee made the selection of the top three submissions based on the playwright's insight regarding family dynamics and caregiving for a person with dementia and ability to convey theme and ideas through character, staging, and dialogue. These three one acts were performed on May 4, 2013 in a staged reading in Asheville, North Carolina. The audience voted on prize ranking with First Place awarded to *Steering Into the Skid* by Deborah Ann Percy and Arnold Johnston, Second Place to *In the Garden* by Matthew Widman, and Third Place to *Riding the Waves* by L.E. Grabowski-Cotton.

In tackling such a difficult subject, one is naturally concerned regarding whether there will be community interest in spending an evening at such a production. It was a magical evening and MemoryCare was utterly grateful for the beautiful rendering of the three plays, the large audience to appreciate them with a standing ovation, and the outpouring of praise that followed. A local theatre professor and playwright wrote, "It is a gracious way to raise consciousness about this issue of memory loss--people will respond to these plays in very positive ways. Art can sometimes reach people when science cannot.[2]" All proceeds from the benefit went to help family caregivers in need of education, training and support.

In a wonderful act of generosity and compassion, these playwrights have agreed to allow MemoryCare to publish their work in this anthology with all proceeds from this book benefiting the families we are privileged to serve every day. In addition, for a period of ten years after the date of this anthology's publication, the playwrights have agreed to allow MemoryCare to grant other nonprofit organizations dedicated to dementia care the same opportunity to utilize their work for educational, advocacy or fundraising events, provided that all profits raised from any such event will be applied to the care or support of persons affected by dementia. Details for non-profits that would like to use the plays as well as discussion questions for each play are provided at the end of this book

Each play in this anthology is introduced by its author. Not surprisingly, each playwright has experienced their own encounters with caregiving. The plays are beautifully crafted and poignantly portray different aspects of the challenges progressive memory disorders pose upon families. From a clinician's perspective, these plays are rich with resources to educate a community; they provide authentic snapshots of how dementia uniquely affects individuals, and powerful testimony to its impact on our most intimate relationships.

Margaret A. Noel, MD

---

[2] (C. Robert Jones, Professor emeritus, Mars Hill University, personal communication, May 5, 2013)

STEERING INTO THE SKID

A Play in Twelve Months

By

Deborah Ann Percy and Arnold Johnston

INTRODUCTION—*Steering into the Skid*

First, we'd like to thank MemoryCare for conceiving the one-act play competition that led to the idea of this book, then for spearheading the successful effort to realize its publication. We'd also like to thank the wonderful performers who read our play at MemoryCare's Night of One Acts, and the director who helped guide them so sensitively in bringing the characters to life.

We actually wrote *Steering into the Skid* prior to seeing MemoryCare's call for plays. We write both full-lengths and one-acts, and we've frequently taught students how to create short plays that actually have a beginning, middle, and end, and lead to a significant change for the characters, rather than just seeming like sketches. Short one-acts, though, usually take place in one scene, often in ten minutes or so of continuous action. With *Skid* we wanted to write a short play that covered an entire year in the lives of its characters, and we decided to use the format of one brief scene per month. Writing a short play with that many scenes flies in the face of conventional playwriting wisdom. But we like a challenge.

And speaking of challenges, growing older has led us to think about the effects of aging on ourselves and our relationship. We've also known friends—couples—who have faced Alzheimer's or other devastating conditions with such dignity, courage, and love that we felt compelled to write about it. So our decisions about form and the facts of our own lives led us to a major decision about content: the significant change for our two characters, Amanda and Tim, would be caused by their advancing age and Tim's subtly developing Alzheimer's, forcing each character to adjust to new demands on their imperfect but loving marriage.

In this play we wanted to create characters an audience cares about first of all because of who they are and how they relate to each other, in the hope that when they are forced to deal with this insidious illness, its impact will be all the more moving. We also believe that even the saddest of experiences should be leavened with humor and that, finally, as E. E. Cummings put it, "Love is the only every god."

—Arnold Johnston & Deborah Ann Percy
Kalamazoo, MI

Arnold Johnston lives in Kalamazoo, MI. His plays, and others written in collaboration with his wife, Deborah Ann Percy, have won awards, production, and publication across the country. His poetry, fiction, non-fiction, and translations have appeared widely in literary journals and anthologies. His books include two poetry collections— *Sonnets: Signs and Portents* and *What the Earth Taught Us*; *The Witching Voice: A Play about Robert Burns*; *Of Earth and Darkness: The Novels of William Golding*; and *The Witching Voice: A Novel from the Life of Robert Burns*. His translations of Jacques Brel's songs have appeared in numerous musical revues nationwide (including the acclaimed Chicago productions *Jacques Brel: Songs of Love and War* and *Jacques Brel's Lonesome Losers of the Night*), and are also featured on his CD, *Jacques Brel: I'm Here!* Commissioned by the Kalamazoo Civic Theatre, Arnie and Debby's interactive drama *The Night Before Christmas* had its highly successful world premiere in December 2012. A performer-singer, Arnie has played many solo concerts and some 100 roles on stage, screen, and radio. He is a member of the Dramatists Guild, The Playwrights' Center, Theatre Communications Group, and the American Literary Translators Association. He was chairman of the English Department (1997-2007) and taught creative writing for many years at Western Michigan University. He is now a full-time writer.

Deborah Ann Percy earned the MFA in Creative Writing at Western Michigan University. A book of her short fiction, *Cool Front: Stories from Lake Michigan*, appeared in 2010 from March Street Press. Her plays, and those written in collaboration with her husband, Arnold Johnston, have won awards, publication, and production nationwide. Their books include their plays *Beyond Sex* and *Rasputin in New York*, a

3

collection of their one-acts, *Duets: Love Is Strange*, and editions (translated with Dona Roşu) of plays by Romanian playwright Hristache Popescu: *Night of the Passions*, *Sons of Cain*, and *Epilogue*. Their edited anthology *The Art of the One Act* appeared in 2007 from New Issues Press. Since 2003 they have written twenty half-hour radio dramas for broadcast on Kalamazoo's NPR-affiliate WMUK-FM as part of *All Ears Theatre*. They've adapted and expanded one of their *All Ears* dramas for the stage, and it appeared in 2013 from Eldridge Publishing as *Rumpelstiltskin: The True Hero*. From 2009-2012 they were joint Arts and Entertainment columnists for the national quarterly journal *Phi Kappa Phi Forum*. After a distinguished administrative career in the Kalamazoo Public Schools, Debby is now a full-time writer. Winner of major playwriting grants from the Michigan Council for Arts & Cultural Affairs and the Irving S. Gilmore Foundation, she is a member of the Dramatists Guild, The Playwrights' Center, and the American Literary Translators Association.

STEERING INTO THE SKID

A Play in Twelve Months

By Deborah Ann Percy and Arnold Johnston

SYNOPSIS

This one-act focuses on Amanda and Tim, both in their sixties, and in twelve short scenes set in their SUV traces a year in their life together from New Year's Day to New Year's Eve. As the months pass, the changes wrought by advancing age and Alzheimer's disease force each character to adjust to new demands on their imperfect but loving marriage.

CHARACTERS

AMANDA: early sixties.

TIM: late sixties.

SETTING

A mid-sized SUV.

TIME

The present, more or less.

NOTE: the set may be minimal, two chairs or cubes to represent car-seats; the actors may mime action and using props, except for the New Year's noisemaker, which is indispensable. Costume changes, too, may be suggested by one or two seasonally appropriate pieces that might be hung on a separate coatrack for each of the two characters. Blackouts between scenes should be unnecessary; that's at the director's discretion, of course, but we'd prefer fluid action.

STEERING INTO THE SKID

A Play in Twelve Months

(As the lights rise, the actors are standing outside their SUV. The time is just after one a.m. on the year's first day.)

AMANDA/TIM: *(In unison, to the audience.)* January.

(AMANDA sits and watches from the front passenger's seat TIM brushes snow from the windshield. She wears a New Year's hat on her head at a jaunty angle. She finally opens the door and blows a party noisemaker at him.)

AMANDA: Tim. That's good enough. Home is only six blocks away. And you've already cleared the side mirrors once.

TIM: I'm almost done. Close the door. You're letting the heat out.

AMANDA: What heat? You haven't even turned on the engine.

TIM: I have to see to drive.

AMANDA: It's freezing.

TIM: Of course it's freezing. Shut the door.

(She does. After a beat, he gets in on the driver's side and throws the scraper on the rear seat. She blows the noisemaker at him again.)

AMANDA: I don't know why you have to be so picky about a little snow on the car.

TIM: It's illegal not to clean your windows. And you know how many drunks are on the road at this time on New Year's Day. Too drunk to clear their windows. They may as well be driving around in igloos.

AMANDA: Igloos don't have windows.

TIM: Exactly.

AMANDA: Why can't you start the car before all the obsessive snow removal?

TIM: If the windows heat up, the snow turns into ice. *(A beat. He turns on the ignition.)*

So much for another Lyle and Libby New Year's Eve party.

AMANDA: Libby told me she's had enough of sex. She says she's too old, and she's done with it.

TIM: *(Driving away.)* Too old? Is there such a thing?

AMANDA: Not from where I sit. She says Lyle keeps harping on it to irritate her.

TIM: Lyle, Lyle, the crocodile. And the woman with the curly red hair. Was she sitting on Lyle's lap all night just to irritate Libby, too?

AMANDA: Rita? You can bet neither the color nor the curls ever occurred in nature. I'm glad we don't have far to go. I'm ready to call it a night. A morning.

TIM: It's not even one o' clock. The New Year's barely started.

AMANDA: I'm tired anyway. And full. Champagne. Filet. And I can still taste the cilantro in those nasty meatballs.

TIM: I'm not tired. We used to stay up a lot later than this. *(Admonishing her.)* Let's not get old.

AMANDA: It's really snowing. Be careful.

TIM: I am being careful.

AMANDA: Tim! Here's our street! Here! Here!

TIM: *(Turning the steering wheel.)* I saw it. You startled me. I could've gone into a skid. You're lucky I know how to steer into them.

AMANDA: You almost missed it, Buster.

TIM: I saw it.

AMANDA: You're just upset because you didn't want to leave the party.

TIM: We used to see the sun come up on January first. Remember?

AMANDA: I remember the hangovers.

TIM: *(Sourly.)* Happy New Year.

AMANDA: I'll sit on your lap.

TIM: Promises, promises.

(She blows the noisemaker at him again. They stand to signal the end of the scene.)

AMANDA/TIM: *(To the audience.)* February.

(TIM sits in the driver's seat, AMANDA in the passenger's. As he mimes driving, AMANDA loosens her coat.)

TIM: *(Tapping the dash.)* Look. Just outside Atlanta and it's already sixty-eight degrees.

AMANDA: It's rush hour. Are we taking the ring road?

TIM: I say straight through. Shoot the rapids.

AMANDA: Atlanta traffic is crazy. How about the ring road?

TIM: How about a snack? A handful of Oat Squares.

AMANDA: Not till you're done shooting the rapids.

TIM: There's a big interchange coming up. Which way do we go?

AMANDA: Left, I think.

TIM: Right here?

AMANDA: Right. No! Go left, right here!

TIM: *(Wrenching on the wheel.)* Good grief, Mandy. First you say left. Then you say right.

AMANDA: I meant you were right—we go left. *(They fall silent for a moment or two.)* Maybe we need a GPS.

TIM: I have all the maps in my head.

AMANDA: Says the man who took us on the unplanned detour through Nashville.

TIM: Says the woman who has an answer for everything.

AMANDA: If we had a GPS, we'd both have an answer for everything.

(They stand to signal the end of the scene.)

AMANDA/TIM: *(To the audience.)* March.

(AMANDA sits in the passenger's seat, watching as TIM finishes scraping the window. He gets in and hooks his seatbelt.)

AMANDA: Meticulous as always.

TIM: We should've stayed in Florida for another month. We could've gone to see the Tigers in Lakeland. They have hitting, pitching, and fielding this season.

AMANDA: You and your Tigers. Should I turn on the GPS?

TIM: I know how to get there. The Best Buy store at the mall. Right?

AMANDA: Do you? It's been a while. Why not use the GPS?

TIM: That expense was your idea. I have the maps in my head, remember?

AMANDA: If we hadn't gotten the GPS, we might still be in Nashville.

TIM: Very funny. I don't like her voice. Mechanical and snotty at the same time.

AMANDA: Change it. Give her a French accent.

TIM: Then I'd have to get used to that. I like things the way they are. There's no reason to change everything.

AMANDA: I'll tell Libby that the next time she talks about dumping Lyle.

TIM: Very funny. I'm serious. This new TV you want. Fifty-inch flat screen. Why do we need a flat screen? The old one's just fine.

AMANDA: This TV is HD—a high-definition picture. You can see individual hairs on people's heads. And DVR. Now you won't miss any baseball games when we go out in the evening.

TIM: DVR. Blu-ray. The Cloud. And these new remotes with new channel numbers. Who can keep track? I can't even figure out which remote to use half the time.

AMANDA: I wrote down all the new cable channels on a notecard.

TIM: *(Grumbling.)* Now all I have to do is keep track of the notecard.

AMANDA: Okay, Buster. Enough crabbing. Start the engine.

TIM: *(Grinning.)* I'll start *you.*

AMANDA: *(Smiling back.)* We live in hope.

(They kiss. Then they stand to signal the end of the scene. They hang up their coats and are dressed for spring.)

AMANDA/TIM: *(To the audience.)* April.

(They sit; TIM is driving, with AMANDA in the passenger's seat.)

TIM: Did you remember the grocery list?

AMANDA: *(Waving it.)* Here it is.

TIM: What time do we have to pick up Jake and the girls?

11

AMANDA: Their plane arrives at two-twenty. In theory.

TIM: Did we remember to put M&M's on the list?

AMANDA: One of us did.

TIM: Oat Squares?

AMANDA: Yep. The ones in the blue box.

TIM: Anything nutritious?

AMANDA: *(Checking the list.)* Not much.

TIM: Good. *(A beat.)* I'm taking the girls to the par-three course tomorrow. Time to start them on golf.

AMANDA: I'll take Jake downtown for lunch. Winfield's.

TIM: The important thing is to practice the swing. Then muscle memory takes over.

AMANDA: Are we talking about golf or sex?

TIM: Very funny. Did you remember the list?

AMANDA: *(After a beat.)* It's right here.

TIM: What about Oat Squares? Did you add Oat Squares?

> *(They stand to signal the end of the scene, then put on something that suggests a social occasion.)*

AMANDA/TIM: *(To the audience.)* May.

> *(They sit. Again, TIM is driving.)*

AMANDA: I could've driven. Let the birthday boy relax and be chauffeured.

TIM: I like driving. May in, May out. *(A beat.)* Where are we going again?

AMANDA: Winfield's. Do you need the GPS?

TIM: I get all the snappy repartee I need without adding her to the mix.

AMANDA: Did you say "snotty"?

TIM: Maybe I should have. At least I didn't say "mechanical."

AMANDA: Lyle said they'd pick up the tab for dinner and dessert. If we want champagne, we'll have to pay for it ourselves.

TIM: Getting the crocodile to pick up any part of a check is satisfaction enough. Does this mean his and Libby's sex life is back on track?

AMANDA: I doubt it. She hid his Viagra.

(They stand to signal the end of the scene. TIM puts on a Detroit Tigers baseball cap.)

AMANDA/TIM: *(To the audience.)* June.

(They sit. TIM is driving, as usual.)

TIM: Poor Lyle. Leg broken in three places?

AMANDA: Perhaps people our age should think twice about taking up parasailing.

TIM: And now he's dependent on Libby for everything.

AMANDA: Not sex, that's for sure.

TIM: We're pretty lucky, aren't we?

AMANDA: Sexwise? Certainly.

TIM: And otherwise. We like each other.

AMANDA: Thank goodness. We all need to remember we could fall off a parasail and find ourselves at the mercy of someone who's profoundly angry at us.

TIM: If you broke your leg in three places, I'd wait on you, hand and injured foot.

AMANDA: I know you would. You're a sweet boy.

TIM: And you are a profoundly sweet girl. But I don't want you waiting on me. Not hand. Not foot.

AMANDA: I know.

TIM: I don't need you laying out my clothes the way you used to do for Jake.

AMANDA: You had on your PJ top. Wouldn't work for dinner, Buddy.

TIM: You're sweet. But I don't need your help.

AMANDA: Speaking of sweet, we need to stop off and pick up a box of chocolates or something for Lyle.

TIM: I guess the aged and infirm revert to childhood tastes. How about a stuffed animal, too?

AMANDA: Be nice, Tim. And stay off parasails.

(They stand to signal the end of the scene, perhaps putting on something summery.)

AMANDA/TIM: *(To the audience.)* July.

(They sit, TIM in the driver's seat.)

AMANDA: Why didn't you just leave the mail in the box till we got back?

TIM: *(Realizing it's in his hand.)* Oh. *(Waving his hand, thinking.)* I . . . I actually . . . I thought you might want something to read along the way.

AMANDA: We're only going to the shoe store to replace your brown loafers. And maybe pick up a birthday gift for Jake.

TIM: *(Starting the car.)* Those loafers were my favorites. Who loses a shoe?

AMANDA: It must've fallen out of the car at the golf course. The day you wore your golf shoes home. That's when you missed it.

TIM: *(Driving.)* And now it's gone. Just plain stupid.

AMANDA: We'll find you an identical pair. *(Looking through the mail.)* Most of this is junk. Credit card offers and insurance stuff. They all want to sell me supplemental Medicare insurance, and I'm not even retired yet.

TIM: They sent me the same crap before I retired. Those shoes were broken in just right.

AMANDA: Like me. Look—even AARP's pushing this stuff. I thought they were on our side.

TIM: *My* side. You're still out every day doing appraisals. Why don't you retire?

AMANDA: We have to pay for things like that flat screen. And Florida.

TIM: *(Waving a brochure.)* They send all this stuff about a vigorous old age, everybody tanned and fit, playing tennis. But they actually think we need protection. A protection racket.

AMANDA: Let's not get old.

TIM: I feel fine.

(They stand to signal the end of the scene.)

AMANDA: *(After a beat, to the audience.)* August.

TIM: August.

(They sit. TIM is driving. A cellphone rings. AMANDA takes it from her purse or a pocket.)

AMANDA: It's Jake. *(Answering.)* Hi, dear. How are you? How's our August birthday girl? Did she like the princess doll? *(Listening, responding cautiously.)* We did. The appointment was at ten.

TIM: *(To the phone.)* Which meant I had to get up way too early.

16

AMANDA: *(Into the phone.)* We're on our way home now. *(Listening.)* No. Not much. No one likes a new doctor, I guess. *(Listening.)* I don't know about costs yet. This guy is the expert on . . .

TIM: *(To the phone, irritably.)* She's dragged me off to an expensive specialist! Because I lost a shoe. Because I can't—don't want to—load the ditchwater. Dishwasher.

AMANDA: *(Into phone, still cautious.)* Can I call you when we get home, honey? Cellphone to cellphone is hard to hear.

TIM: And too easy for me to hear!

AMANDA: *(Into phone.)* I love you, too. Kiss the girls for us. I'll call you back in an hour or so.

TIM: *(To the phone.)* When I'm not around to hear!

AMANDA: *(Closing phone; then to TIM.)* Sweetheart. Buddy.

TIM: I don't like any of this.

AMANDA: I don't like it either. I don't.

TIM: Let's make it go away. Let's go away. Let's take off for Florida. See the Tigers in . . .

AMANDA: Lakeland.

TIM: This damn RPM could get us there.

AMANDA: GPS, sweetie.

TIM: GPS.

AMANDA: We had a lovely time, didn't we? Walking on the beach. Eating grouper bites.

TIM: A lovely time? Grouper bites?

AMANDA: In Florida.

TIM: Right. In Florida.

(They stand to signal the end of the scene and put on something to suggest fall.)

AMANDA: *(After a beat, to the audience.)* September.

(They sit in their usual places, with TIM driving.)

TIM: Is it Winfield's?

AMANDA: That's right, sweetie. Libby's favorite place. Ours, too, remember?

TIM: Of course I remember.

AMANDA: And I DVR-ed the Tigers game so you won't miss it.

TIM: Hitting. Pitching. *(A beat.)* DVR-ed. *(A beat.)* Good. Good work, Mandy.

AMANDA: You can watch it when we get home from dinner.

TIM: At Winfield's.

AMANDA: Right. With Libby.

TIM: What I don't understand is why she would want me along.

AMANDA: We come as a set, don't we? And she can use the moral support.

TIM: Who gets divorced in their sixties?

AMANDA: Everyone has some sort of limit. She's rediscovered her sex drive.

TIM: And what about Lyle?

AMANDA: He's rediscovered the chemically-enhanced redhead.

TIM: I guess he must have found his Viagra.

AMANDA: Did you take *your* pills today?

TIM: Viagra?

AMANDA: Tim. You know what I mean.

TIM: I forgot. I'll wash them down with champagne at . . .

AMANDA: *(Seeing he's at a loss.)* Winfield's. Turn here. Right here. Turn right.

> *(They stand to signal the end of the scene. TIM puts on a pair of glasses, which he'll wear for the rest of the play.)*

AMANDA: *(To the audience.)* October. *(TIM sits, staring straight ahead. AMANDA, standing, knocks on the window.)* Roll it down! The button's right there. *(Startled, he pushes a button.)* Why are you sitting out here in the driveway?

TIM: The driveway?

AMANDA: That's right. The driveway.

TIM: Mandy. I couldn't find the golf course.

AMANDA: Tim. Sweetie. It's in the GPS. In "Favorites."

TIM: I turned it on. She wouldn't say a word, snotty or otherwise.

AMANDA: She doesn't talk till she knows where you want to go.

TIM: I had no idea where I was. So I just drove around. Then I saw our mailbox.

AMANDA: *(After a beat.)* Come on in. It's time for lunch.

TIM: Do we have Oat Squares?

AMANDA: It's too cold for golf anyway. Come on inside, Buster. *(They stand to signal the end of the scene and put on fall coats. She speaks to the audience.)* November.

(Both are standing outside the SUV.)

TIM: What's this guy's name? This twerp?

AMANDA: Doctor Antwerp.

TIM: See. I knew he was some kind of twerp.

AMANDA: *(Trying for lightness.)* And he speaks so well of you.

TIM: *(A beat.)* Tell me this, Amanda. Why aren't you going to retire now? We planned it all out.

AMANDA: Plans change, buddy. *(They stand to signal the end of the scene and put on something to suggest a party. She speaks to the audience.)* December. *(TIM sits on the passenger's side while AMANDA brushes snow* *off the windshield. She opens the door and leans toward him.)* You look frozen. Should I start the car so it can warm up?

TIM: That'll make the windows ice up.

AMANDA: Right you are, sweetie. I'll be done in a second. *(She closes the door and leans on the car's roof for a moment.)* Oh, Tim. Buddy. *(She finishes brushing the windshield and gets into the driver's seat. She closes the door, tosses the scraper onto the rear seat, and hooks her seatbelt.)* So. Are you all ready for Libby's first solo New Year's Eve party?

TIM: Where's Lyle the . . . the . . .

AMANDA: Crocodile? Sunning himself on a riverbank, for all I know.

TIM: I still don't see why I have to have a visiting nurse. *(Pointing at the GPS.)* It'll be like having *her* in the house. She's bad enough in the car.

AMANDA: It'll let you stay at home without my worrying. Otherwise, you'd have to be . . .

TIM: *(Cutting her off.)* Why can't you just call me now and again from work like you do now? I take my pills, just the way I'm supposed to.

AMANDA: You know how busy I get at work, especially when I'm out doing appraisals. I'd hate to forget and leave you sitting home with no one to talk to.

TIM: I don't want someone snotty and mechanical. I want *you.*

AMANDA: We'll find somebody nice. I promise. Anyway, right now we're going to Libby's party. We'll have a good time.

21

TIM: I can drive.

AMANDA: I know.

TIM: I *like* to drive.

AMANDA: I know, Buddy.

TIM: You don't really care for her—what is it?—meatballs.

AMANDA: *(Pleased.)* Oh, you remember. Her meatballs are really nasty. Too much garlic. And cilantro. Who puts half a cup of cilantro in meatballs?

TIM: I can drive. I *like* to drive.

AMANDA: I know. *(After a beat.)* We'll find someone good to come and spend time with you.

TIM: I feel like I'm moving inside an igloo. Snow all around me. *(She looks at him, unable to reply. After a beat, he holds up the party noisemaker from the opening scene.)* I found this under the seat. What is it?

> *(She takes it from him gently and blows it at him, then kisses his cheek as the lights fade to black.)*

END

IN THE GARDEN

A Play in One Act

By

Matthew Widman

INTRODUCTION—*In the Garden*

When my oldest daughter Mariah was two years old, we frequently travelled across the river for the day to my father's childhood home in New Jersey to take care of my grandmother, who was then in the middle stages of Alzheimer's disease. Ever since I could remember, Julia had been an extremely dignified and reserved white-haired Italian woman who had always kept an immaculate house and had little patience for, or interest in young children. But everything changed with her illness. If there was a silver lining to the disease, it came with my grandmother's newly open and carefree attitude and a special fascination with her very young great granddaughter. I remember one particularly poignant moment when Nana and Mariah were both arguing passionately over a tiny ceramic bell. It was a tchotchke that my grandmother had picked up on a trip abroad and placed on a shelf where it had sat untouched for decades. But now the bell was a shiny prize lying out on the ottoman, a jiggling bone of contention for two minds passing in opposite directions. It was the most human but plaintive of moments, the nexus of lives eighty-five years apart connecting, thinking and relating in harmony, one mind brimming with hope and potential, the other robbed of its sense of self by a brutal disease, on its way in full decline toward a world beyond understanding.

In the Garden is dedicated to my father Harry Widman, a wonderful artist, teacher and parent. Although the characters in this play are fictional, my father's aesthetic voice rings true through the persona of Arthur, a man who despite his illness, never loses his observant eye for the splendor and the excitement of the world around him. If artists are interpreters, filtering the world through their senses and translating it into their medium, then it is the subversive nature of Alzheimer's to constantly strip away at memory, a crucial mediator of perception, and deprive the artistic mind of its bearings. For my father, heading into the later stages of the disease, his is a new and elusive reality that I can only image. And for his friends and loved ones, we are forced to come to terms with our ever-shifting reality as

24

well—that of the changing essence of the person we once knew and continue to love. His wife Mardy has been heroic in her caregiving, reconciling the challenging personality swings and memory loss while enjoying my father's periods of lucidity and engagement and cherishing their common history together. Her workload is tremendous, compensated by occasional moments of levity or insight as she strives to maintain the best possible quality of life for my father over the final slow and difficult journey.

In telling the story of the Monsetin family in their moment of crisis, *In the Garden* tries to address the terrible impact of Alzheimer's and dementia—what it does to those stricken, both mentally and physically, and the immense challenges and pressures that it places on the caretakers. But so much of what is both tragic and human about this condition is beyond simple clinical description, lying in the margins of human understanding and explanation. *In the Garden* touches on some of the more philosophical questions that the disease elicits, not the least of which is to ask what comprises the *essence* of a person? What defines a *self*? What defines *normal*? Is there credence or value in differing views of external reality? How does memory define who we are in the moment? These are questions that my father, a great reader of plays and a man who valued highly both the rational mind and his sense of human dignity, would very much appreciate.

I would like to thank Dr. Margaret Noel and MemoryCare for the opportunity to address Alzheimer's disease through the lens of theater and the arts, and to extend an additional thank you to all who participated in and made the Spring, 2013, Asheville readings possible. Alzheimer's is a leveling disease, attacking and scrambling the neural connections regardless of wealth, culture, sex, race or creed. Without mitigation or cure, the only current "treatment" for this terminal condition is direct caregiving—the ceaseless attention from one human being to another. As our society ages and Alzheimer's disease and dementia reach epidemic proportions, MemoryCare and other support organizations become invaluable links to helping us all better understand this illness and plan strategies to cope with its devastating effects. But, most importantly, for those enveloped in a difficult Alzheimer's world that can quietly devolve into isolation and despair, MemoryCare and other dedicated groups and organizations offer the most vital of services - comfort, care and community.

—Matthew Widman
New York, New York

Matthew Widman has written multiple stage plays, screenplays and short stories. *Kill the Dog,* Widman's full-length black comedy, was selected as one of the top ten finalists for the Bloomington Playwrights Project's Reva Shiner Comedy Award. Widman's short comedic play *Dinner Knight* was produced as part of the HB Playwrights Foundation's *Kitchen Plays* festival in New York and his comedic adaptation *Unlikely Affair* (commissioned, Hapi Feet Inc., Frank Leahy, Prod.) has been performed on numerous stages throughout Canada. His short dramatic play *Life of the Party* was chosen as a finalist by the Actors Theatre of Louisville for their National Ten-Minute Play Contest's Heideman Award. Widman's screenplay, *The Gospel of Now* was named as a quarterfinalist in the Nicholl Fellowship Screenwriting Competition and his short story *In the Woods* was chosen as a finalist in the America's Best Competition for Short Fiction. A native of Portland, Oregon, Matt Widman graduated from Williams College, attended the Columbia University Writing Program and is a member of Donna de Matteo's Playwriting Workshop at HB Studio in New York City. In addition to his longtime association with St. Nicholas Music, Inc., Widman has worked for years in film and television production on both large studio movies and on smaller independent projects and documentaries. He currently lives in Greenwich Village with his wife and children.

IN THE GARDEN

By Matthew Widman

SYNOPSIS

The Monsetin family is in crisis. Beloved father Arthur is fighting a losing battle with Alzheimer's disease and his three grown children, Peter, Karen and Jamie have gathered at the family house to decide what to do. But the choices are not easy. While Arthur may wander off at times, or lash out in anger or forget the names of his grandchildren, at other times he is lucid, funny and wise. Long ingrained familial tensions boil to the surface as Peter, Karen and Jamie struggle to treasure their father's last cogent moments before he is lost to them forever.

CHARACTERS

ARTHUR MONSETIN: 78, retired professor and artist, a gentleman who manages to maintain his underlying dignity despite his disease

PETER MONSETIN: 38, Arthur's older son

KAREN MONSETIN: 35, Arthur's daughter

JAMIE MONSETIN: 32, Arthur's younger son

SETTING

In and around the suburban California Monsetin house. The action takes place in the living room and kitchen, in Arthur's bedroom, in the backyard garden and in the surrounding neighborhood.

TIME

The present. The story takes place over three days.

IN THE GARDEN

(The stage is dark. There is a garden bench and a garden chair down C facing us. This is THE GARDEN. When lights are up on the garden, we hear the sounds of nature. Up R is an end table with a lamp and a living room couch facing the cluttered counter of a connected kitchen. This is THE LIVING ROOM and THE KITCHEN. Up L are a large wooden bureau and a chair. Knickknacks clutter the top of the bureau and surround a framed portrait of ARTHUR and VIVIAN. An umbrella leans against the bureau. Next to the bureau, the chair is piled high with men's clothing. A bright woman's V-neck sweater and a purse hang over the back of the chair. This is THE BEDROOM. The action will occur in these three settings and in the empty spaces down L and R of THE GARDEN.)

(Lights fade up in THE BEDROOM. ARTHUR MONSETIN stands at the bureau wearing a dark sweatshirt, pajama pants and sneakers. He is very busy at the bureau, opening and closing drawers, rearranging everything. He opens the top drawer, takes out a deck of cards, puts it on top of the bureau. He opens a lower drawer, takes two apples out of each of his pajama pockets and puts them in the drawer. He moves over to the pile of clothes on the chair, pulls a sweatshirt on over the sweatshirt he's already wearing. He tucks his pajama pants high up over his sweatshirts.)

ARTHUR: *(Berating himself.)* No, no, you *dumbhead*. *(He takes a wrench from the top of the bureau, puts it in his pocket. He takes some batteries, puts them in his pocket. As he talks to himself, he takes a metal Altoid candy box out of his pocket, fills it up with loose change from the top of the bureau.)* I want to go downtown—get some cash. Cash into money. Not an awful lot . . . just in case I need it. I'm a poor man, you know. Need money in my pocket.

28

(ARTHUR shakes the Altoid box, listens to the rattling coins. Satisfied, he puts the box in his pocket, carefully closes all the bureau drawers. He picks up the umbrella leaning against the bureau, exits the bedroom. The bedroom goes dark.)

(Everything is black except for a small spot of light downstage. Off L and off R we hear the voices of PETER MONSETIN and JAMIE MONSETIN calling Arthur's name as they approach the stage.)

JAMIE: *(Off, calling loudly.)* Arthur! Arthur! Arthur Monsetin!

PETER: *(Off, calling, worried.)* Dad! Arthur! Where are you?

JAMIE: *(Off.)* Dad! Dad, it's Jamie! Dad!

PETER: *(Off.)* Arthur Monsetin! Can you hear me? It's Peter, Dad! It's Peter!

(PETER and JAMIE continue calling until they converge onstage, meet in the spot of light. PETER wears khakis and a polo shirt. JAMIE is dressed in cargo shorts, a tee shirt and sandals. As they talk, they look out and around them, searching for Arthur.)

JAMIE: I went by the park, checked all the benches. Did you find anything?

PETER: He could be anywhere. I asked everyone I saw. We should probably get the car. *(Harsh.)* I thought you were watching him.

JAMIE: I *was* watching him. He was in the living room. Then he went into the bedroom. I thought he was going to take a nap. You know how he just kind of sleeps whenever he's tired now—or just goes out into the garden.

29

PETER: Did you even bother to check?

JAMIE: He's a grown man. What am I supposed to tell him? That he can't go where he wants? Then he yells at me. It's his house.

PETER: You're supposed to be grown man, too. You were on duty. You're supposed to keep him from wandering off. At least for two more days.

JAMIE: Hey, I talk to him all the time, and he's not as bad as you and Karen think. I was telling him about meditation the other day and he was really getting into it. I think he's starting to remember more.

PETER: Do you know anything? Have you even bothered to read any of the links I've been sending you? *(To a child.)* It's not a cold. It's *Alzheimer's*. He doesn't get better.

JAMIE: I know you think I'm an idiot, but you're not the only one who reads. I fixed him a blueberry and ginger smoothie yesterday. I'm telling you, his mind was much sharper after that. He told me all about his sledding accident when he was eight. *(Pointing.)* Did you know he lost these two teeth?

PETER: Was he wearing his ID bracelet? Karen told me he cut the last one off.

JAMIE: ID bracelet ?

PETER: *(Annoyed.)* The green band. With his name and phone number on it.

JAMIE: I don't know, probably. I mean, it was hard to tell, he had on, like, three sweatshirts.

30

PETER: You're unbelievable. He could be walking down the middle of the highway. If anything happens to him it's going to be your fault.

JAMIE: I had to go to the bathroom, alright? *(Softly.)* He's probably out looking for Mom.

(PETER'S cell phone RINGS. PETER answers.)

PETER: *(Into the phone.)* Hi. Did you find him? . . . You did! Great, where was he? . . . You're kidding . . . Okay, see you in a few minutes. Bye. *(To Jamie.)* You know that red house on Pine Street, by the corner of Bison? He was on their porch swing. Good thing for you he had his bracelet on.

JAMIE: You know, man, Dad's happy. He's more at peace than he's been in years. He might not remember things, but you could learn a little about kicking back from him.

PETER: Well good, I'm glad he's relaxed. He deserves it. He *worked* all his life. He worked hard. Maybe *you* could learn a little from him about *that.*

JAMIE: Yeah, well I don't need money to be happy. I'm *good.* *(A dig.)* I don't have a big fat alimony bill coming like some people.

PETER: *(Hard.)* No, you don't have that, do you? You really don't have much of anything. *(Turning away.)* I'm going back this way.

JAMIE: I think I'll take the scenic route.

(They exit in opposite directions. The stage goes black.)

31

(Lights up on THE LIVING ROOM. Arthur sits on the couch. He's facing KAREN MONSETIN at the kitchen counter pouring a glass of water from a pitcher.)

KAREN: Can I get you a glass of cold water, Dad?

ARTHUR: No, no, I don't think so.

KAREN: You don't want to get dehydrated. You know how you forget to drink. And you should probably take your pills.

ARTHUR: Vivian should be home soon.

KAREN: *(Deep breath.)* Mom's away for a while. Were you looking for Mom? Is that why you went on your walk?

ARTHUR: My walk?

KAREN: At least it's a nice day out.

(ARTHUR stands, confused in the moment, examines KAREN.)

ARTHUR: *Vivian?*

(KAREN puts a glass of water on the end table, gently guides ARTHUR back down onto the couch.)

KAREN: Mom's not here, Dad. Sit down, have some water. I'm Karen.

ARTHUR: Yes, I know you.

KAREN: I'm your daughter.

ARTHUR: Karen, I know. Karen in college.

KAREN: No, I'm not in college anymore. I finished college. I live here now, nearby. About five miles away. With Eric, my husband. Do you remember Eric?

ARTHUR: Eric? No, no, I can't say I know him.

KAREN: And Ruby and Colin, your grandchildren. Remember they were visiting yesterday?

ARTHUR: Is that so. And where do they live?

KAREN: With me, Dad. And Eric.

ARTHUR: *Eric? Eric?* I'm sorry, that doesn't ring a bell. Have you seen Vivian? She may be upstairs.

KAREN: Dad, it's time for your pills.

ARTHUR: Pills?

KAREN: For your heart. Your cholesterol. You just need to swallow them.

ARTHUR: I think I have to go home. Vivian's at home. I think I have to go.

> *(ARTHUR starts to rise. KAREN puts a calming hand on his shoulder, gently dissuades him.)*

KAREN: Dad, you *are* at home. This is your house. You've lived here for fifty years.

ARTHUR: I have?

KAREN: *(Hands him a pill.)* Please, take this one.

ARTHUR: *(Holds up the pill, examining.)* This pill. You want me to take *this* pill. This little thing. This little object. You say this is useful.

KAREN: It's good for your health.

ARTHUR: Well, okay then.

(ARTHUR takes the Altoid box out of his pocket. Puts the pill in box. Puts the   box back in his pocket.)

KAREN: Dad, you have to take it. And there are two more.

ARTHUR: I don't think I want to take it right now. I'll take it later.

KAREN: *(In frustration.)* Dad!

ARTHUR: *(Forceful.)* Karen, I said I will take it later.

KAREN: *(Giving up.)* Well, at least have some water.

ARTHUR: I don't want any water.

KAREN: *(Pause, with difficulty.)* Listen, I need to talk to you about something. *(Deep breath.)* What would you think about moving? Maybe going to a place that's more social. More people around. Don't you think you might like that?

(ARTHUR'S looking down the side of the couch.)

ARTHUR: Oh, ho . . . look who we have here.

(He picks up a stuffed dog.)

KAREN: You found Aldo! Ruby's been looking everywhere. She was so upset last night when she couldn't find him.

(ARTHUR holds up the dog, inspects it.)

ARTHUR: He's a fine creature.

KAREN: Aldo is Ruby's best friend . . . *(Holds out her hand.)* Could I . . . could I please see the dog?

ARTHUR: *(Stands, matter-of-factly.)* Well, I think I'm ready. *(Tucks the dog under his arm.)* It was very nice to visit with you.

(Arthur exits.)

KAREN: *(Calling after him.)* Dad. Dad, I'm going to need to get Aldo back before I go home . . .

(The living room goes black.)

(Lights up on THE GARDEN. ARTHUR sits in the garden chair facing us. He holds the stuffed dog, looks out, admires what he sees. PETER sits across from ARTHUR on the bench, also facing us.)

ARTHUR: *(Basking.)* This is a beautiful place. Just being here is quite wonderful . . . *(A moment, then he leans over, looks PETER affectionately in the eye.)* It's a pleasure, a pleasure to sit with you—here, in the garden.

PETER: It's a pleasure to be here with you too, Dad. Are you still painting? You always said how much you love to paint outside. The flowers and the trees and—*(Gazing upward.)*—the sky.

ARTHUR: *(Looking up.)* Yes, that sky, so blue . . .

PETER: Remember how you retired from teaching to have more time for your art? I mean, I don't know much about painting, but you were getting pretty good.

35

ARTHUR: *(Pause, then suddenly clued in, cogent.)* I was still learning very basic stuff . . . adapting in my head as I went along.

PETER: You loved it. And you worked really hard to get better.

ARTHUR: *(Reflecting.)* I began to understand which were the things I'd done the day before that might work . . . *(Looking up at the sky again.)* As I say that I see that blue sky and it's beautiful—nature adjusting itself. Not so exciting that it's going to change your life, but you're going to see things that you haven't seen before . . .

PETER: Maybe it's not nature that's adjusting—maybe you were the one adjusting.

ARTHUR: *(Nodding, animated now.)* For an artist that's what it's all about . . . *(Gesturing, back in the classroom.)* What would happen if the red in that flower were violet? Would it still affect you? It's an internal game that you play. You can play it without knowing if there's really something there . . . *(Gesturing.)* I get awfully jealous of that green bush. See it there, against that gorgeous blue?—*spectacular* . . . there's *value* in such things. *(Gesturing back to the flowers.)* Those flowers, if that red isn't right, then by god I'm going to fix that red so it is right . . . *(Suddenly self-conscious.)* Now I'm going to be quiet. *(Pause, then can't contain himself.)* We're all living in this environment. Everything here. And we can select out of this environment whatever we want to select—*(Pointing out.)*—and by god there are those red flowers again—but then I look over there and there are those yellow guys and they're alive too . . . *(Quiet awe, very self-aware.)* It's crazy stuff that I see . . . but I'm going to shut up now. I'm just talking.

PETER: That's okay, Dad, I like hearing you talk. I always wish I could have taken one of your classes.

36

ARTHUR: *(Smiling gently.)* To carry this silly conversation a little longer—*(Passionate again, an art lecture.)*—as an artist, *bang*, you have an insight. We have a certain kind of knowledge with us all the time that has meaning, many different kinds of meaning. It's wondrous things that we see because we haven't seen them before . . . that's exciting, seeing it while you're doing it in a way that's new. What we take in instantaneously, superficially, we have to stop to look at more closely . . . *(Pointing to the treetops.)* I can choose to see the blue sky or the tree. If I chose to see the tree, I have to make adjustments in my brain . . . I'm just talking . . . But it's really intriguing to look at these things and try to make your own way of thinking. That dark tree— cut out of the blue to make a thing that I see, or something I *believe* I see—what I'm saying is an *interpretation*. It's about *interpretation*. It's kind of like seeing something again that you've looked at for a very long time—but hadn't *really* seen.

(Karen enters. She carries a stuffed pig.)

KAREN: There you two are. *(She kisses ARTHUR.)* Hi, Dad.

PETER: *(To ARTHUR.)* It's Karen.

ARTHUR: *(Warmly.)* Karen. Do we have to worry about you?

KAREN: I'm your daughter, you always have to worry about me. Did I interrupt a heavy conversation?

PETER: Dad was just telling me about his art.

KAREN: He's got some nice paintings up in the attic. *(To ARTHUR.)* You have some nice paintings up in the attic playroom, Dad.

PETER: New ones?

37

KAREN: No, I think you may have seen them. They're a couple of years old. I don't think he's been able to focus much on his art lately.

(ARTHUR points to the stuffed pig KAREN'S holding.)

ARTHUR: I like your friend there.

KAREN: Oh, good. I was thinking maybe we could trade. I have to go home and make a meal for everyone. Eric's been great, but I feel like we haven't had any family time in weeks. I just have to go.

PETER: *(Encouraging.)* Yeah, sure, go home. Everything will be fine. I'm happy to be here, get out of that Marriott.

KAREN: But I have to bring Ruby back her dog. She's going to be so upset if she doesn't have Aldo again tonight. *(To ARTHUR.)* Dad, can we trade? Can I give you this pig and get Ruby's dog back?

(ARTHUR pulls away. Clutches the dog, suddenly hostile.)

ARTHUR: What? You mean *this* dog? You mean *my* dog?

PETER: Actually, Dad, it's Ruby's dog.

ARTHUR: Ruby? Who's Ruby?

PETER: Ruby's your granddaughter.

ARTHUR: *(To himself, disbelief.)* My granddaughter. My granddaughter. You're saying I have a *granddaughter?* No. No. No. No.

KAREN: Dad, please. Take it. It's a really nice pig.

ARTHUR: *(Stern.)* You want to take away my dog, I said *no*.

KAREN: Please, Dad. Can't you just give me the dog?

38

ARTHUR: *Vivian*, do you know what *no* means? It means *no*. No, *Vivian*, no.

KAREN: *(Upset.)* I'm not *Vivian*. I'm Karen—I'm Karen, your daughter. I'm not your wife. *(Holds the pig out to Arthur, losing it.)* Just take the pig. *(ARTHUR grabs the pig.)* I've got to get out of here.

(KAREN quickly exits.)

PETER: *(Standing.)* Karen, wait.

(PETER quickly follows her out. ARTHUR watches them go without emotion, tucks the pig under his arm together with the stuffed dog. Satisfied, he settles back in his chair, gazes serenely out over the garden. Fade to black.)

(Lights up on JAMIE in THE BEDROOM. He's searching through the top bureau drawer. He finds an old wallet, takes out some bills, puts the money in his pocket. He spots the purse hanging on the chair. He puts the wallet back in the drawer and closes it. He opens the purse, rifles through it, finds a small change purse inside. He takes some cash out of the change purse, puts it in his pocket. He searches again in the purse, holds up a woman's pedant watch on a chain. JAMIE dangles the watch, contemplates it for a long moment. Then he presses the watch against his cheek, closes his eyes. Blackout.)

(Lights up on KAREN and PETER at THE KITCHEN counter. As they talk, they unload two bags of groceries.)

PETER: He slept with Aldo last night. I don't think he's let go of that stuffed dog for a minute. But sooner or later he'll put it down and forget—then I'll get it back for you. Was Ruby okay?

KAREN: No. Not really. Not after everything with Mom. Nobody's really okay. There's just too much stress. She's only four. She wants to know why I'm never home, and then when she's here with me she's scared of Dad. And Colin—two-year-olds have so much energy—he's running off in one direction and Dad's going in another . . . (*Disheartened.*) Eric's already taken all his vacation days for the year . . . (*Pause, torn.*) I still don't know if we're making the right decision.

PETER: Karen, listen to yourself, you need to get your life back.

KAREN: I just think it might be too much for him all at once.

PETER: For him, time doesn't matter anymore. Every day is new. We've been talking about this for months. What choice do we have? (*Disparaging.*) Jamie keeps telling me we should hire someone again to come in and help out. But that's Jamie—he wants to keep sleeping until eleven o'clock every morning.

KAREN: You know, you can be a little hard on him. Jamie means well. And he's been pretty good with Dad.

PETER: (*Pause.*) I don't think in-home's an option anymore. It sounds like the nurse was a disaster.

KAREN: It got really bad. You know how awkward Dad's always been with strangers. I think the disease has made him worse. He would yell at the poor woman anytime she came near him. I was even worried he might maybe, I don't know, hit her. He just got so hostile.

PETER: (*Sadly.*) That's hard to believe . . . he was always such a pussycat.

(Pause.)

KAREN: It's not *him*. I mean, it *is* him—but it's not *really* him anymore.

(Pause.)

PETER: So what do you think about Sunday?

KAREN: I don't know. I talked to Eric about it. He said if it were him, no matter *what* his state of mind, he would want to know. And he's probably right.

PETER: The whole thing could totally set Dad off. *(KAREN looks away, nods silently.)* Well, we should decide by tomorrow. Either way it's going to be rough.

(They are quiet for a moment as they put the last of the groceries away.)

KAREN: I'm sorry things didn't work out with Jen. I really liked her.

PETER: I know. I liked her too. But she didn't like me. That's the way the world is sometimes.

KAREN: *(Pause)* Yeah. That's the way the world is. But I'm still sorry.

(KAREN wraps her arms around PETER and hugs him. They stand together like this as lights slowly fade.)

(Lights up on THE GARDEN. ARTHUR sits facing us, holds the stuffed dog, admires the garden. ARTHUR'S pajama pants are tucked up over his fleece jacket. JAMIE sits next to him on the bench. He has a chime instrument on his lap. The garden chair is empty.)

41

JAMIE: So I was thinking about massage therapy. That would be a good career.

ARTHUR: It sounds very good.

JAMIE: I could take classes downtown. It only costs about six hundred dollars.

ARTHUR: Yes, money. Money, money, money makes the world go round.

JAMIE: Hey, Dad, listen to this.

(He taps the chime. A soothing gong sound.)

ARTHUR: Oh, did you do that?

JAMIE: That's nice, huh? I'm realigning your chakra. The one for memory. *(He taps on the chime again. ARTHUR closes his eyes. Then JAMIE hits a different TONE. ARTHUR opens his eyes, looks up at the sky.)* That one was for Mom.

ARTHUR: *(Staring up.)* There's that sky that I'm so jealous of, just spreading out and covering the world.

JAMIE*: (Looking up.)* Yeah, that's really something ...

ARTHUR: *That beautiful sky.*

JAMIE: Hey, Dad, is it okay if I borrow some money? I found some in your bedroom.

ARTHUR: *(Still looking up)* Money, money, money. We all need money.

JAMIE: Thanks, Dad. *(He looks a little closer at ARTHUR'S lap.)* Whoops. Looks like you had a little accident there.

ARTHUR: What's that?

JAMIE: I think you might have wet yourself.

ARTHUR: *(Looks down, examining, annoyed.)* I don't think so.

JAMIE: *(Pause, shrugs.)* Okay, sure, whatever. *(Standing.)* I'm going to go get a beer. You want one?

> *(ARTHUR doesn't answer. JAMIE waits a moment, then exits. ARTHUR stares back up at the sky. Blackout.)*

> *(The stage is dark. It's night, very late. Then a light goes on in THE KITCHEN. Then some drawers bang as ARTHUR, fully dressed, pulls out a steak knife. He wears VIVIAN'S brightly colored V-neck sweater over his sweatshirt. His pajama pants are tucked up high over both. ARTHUR holds up the steak knife and examines it. Still holding the knife, ARTHUR takes out a plate, drops it with a clatter down on the counter. He takes out a second plate, puts it down on the counter also with a clatter. He goes to a fruit bowl, takes out a banana, lays it down on one of the plates. Methodically, ARTHUR begins to cut the skin off the banana. On the couch, rumbled blankets begin to move. PETER reaches up, turns on the light.)*

PETER: *(On the couch, groggy.)* Who is that? Is that you, Dad?

ARTHUR: *(Cheerfully.)* Hello. That's me.

PETER: What are you doing?

ARTHUR: Just making a little breakfast.

43

PETER: But it's two in the morning. It's the middle of the night. *(ARTHUR doesn't respond. Hums as he works. PETER groans, gets up off the couch. He's wearing undershorts and a tee shirt. He joins his father at the counter.)* What are you making?

ARTHUR: Oh, just a little banana.

PETER: *(Looking over his shoulder.)* You're quite the chef. Why are you cutting out all the seeds? You can eat those, you know.

ARTHUR: I don't think they're good.

(PETER picks up one of the plates off the counter.)

PETER: Well, it's a little too early for my breakfast. I think I'll put this one back.

ARTHUR: *(Jolted.)* No. That's Vivian's plate.

(PETER puts the plate back down.)

PETER: *(Pause, with difficulty.)* Dad, Mom is . . . Mom's *away.* She won't be here for breakfast. *(ARTHUR drops the knife on the plate. Starts to exit the kitchen.)* Wait, Dad, where are you going?

ARTHUR: I have to go home now. I get tired of all this.

PETER: Hey Dad, wait. Wait, do you . . . *(Searching.)* How about watching a baseball game? Do you want to watch baseball?

(ARTHUR returns to the counter.)

ARTHUR: Baseball? Sure, that could be all right.

PETER: The Dodgers. Do you still like the Dodgers?

44

ARTHUR: Ah, the *Dodgers.*

PETER: I'll check on the TV. We can watch a game tomorrow. Wouldn't that be good?

ARTHUR: Sure, sounds good.

(*PETER motions to the couch.*)

PETER: It's really late. Why don't you come sit down?

ARTHUR: No, no, I think I'll make a little breakfast . . . (*He sees the cut banana on the plate.*) Oh, I see somebody's already started.

PETER: That's okay. That's for you.

ARTHUR: (*Pleased.*) Very good . . . very good.

(*ARTHUR resumes cutting the banana. PETER joins him at the counter, watches him as he works.*)

PETER: How are you feeling, Dad? Are you doing okay?

ARTHUR: Oh, still staggering around trying to get myself together. I don't admit it, of course—(*Joking, conspiratorially.*)—except to a close friend.

PETER: We're all staggering. Maybe that's just the natural state of things, you know? Maybe doing well is the exception . . . (*Pause.*) I thought I'd have a family by now. I have a son. Your grandson Benjamin. But I don't have a family anymore . . . (*Pause.*) Was it hard? When we were kids?

(*ARTHUR stops cutting. Contemplates.*)

45

ARTHUR: The *kids*. The kids were kind of mixed into a lot of things. Or *I* was mixed into a lot of things. Kids made things complicated —but also opened things up. There were no clear answers—*(He puts a hand on Peter's shoulder. Looks at him kindly. A father again.)*—there were never "for sures"—there were just efforts to get on through—to the next problem.

PETER: Jennifer left me a couple of months ago. She's got Benjamin. She said to tell you hello—and how sorry she is.

ARTHUR: Who's that?

PETER: Jennifer, my wife. Or she was my wife. Do you remember our wedding?

ARTHUR: No. No, I can't say that I do.

PETER: You gave a great toast. So did Mom. Jen wanted to come Sunday. I told her not to.

ARTHUR: I guess I'm not familiar with what's happening Sunday.

PETER: *(Pause, weighing.)* We're having a . . . *a party.* A sad party.

ARTHUR: And you'll be there.

PETER: Yes, I'll be there.

ARTHUR: *(Pause.)* I'm sorry, could you tell me your name again?

PETER: *(Pause, deflated.)* It's Peter, Dad, your oldest son. You have three children. Me, Karen and Jamie. Remember?

ARTHUR: No. No, I guess I didn't know that.

PETER: Are you getting tired? It's really late.

ARTHUR: No. No, I think I'll just be right here.

PETER: Okay. Is it alright if I go back to sleep?

ARTHUR: Sure, sure, I'm going to work a little more.

(PETER goes to the couch, lies back down, turns off the light. ARTHUR tears a napkin into strips. Begins to carefully wrap each banana slice into a napkin strip. Fade to black.)

(Lights fade up on JAMIE and KAREN in THE GARDEN. They are sitting together on the bench.)

JAMIE: *(Sadly.)* Karen, you can't sell the house. Mom did so much work on this garden. Since we were kids . . . *(Pause.)* Remember when she got Dad to put in the birdbath and he threw out his back for, like, a month?

KAREN: *(Smiling.)* Are you kidding? Do you think Dad would ever let us forget that? He could be a pretty good complainer.

JAMIE: Yeah, but a lot of it was just to bug Mom.

KAREN: And she thought it was funny. That drove me crazy. She was amazing.

JAMIE: Why did she ever marry Dad? *(Pause.)* But I guess she knew what she was getting into.

KAREN: I don't know. How do you ever know what you're getting with another person? *In sickness and in health.* I think you just have to be really, really lucky.

JAMIE: Like you and Eric.

KAREN: *(Pause.) Maybe.*

JAMIE: *(Pause.)* Dad was lucky.

KAREN: All three of us were lucky.

(Pause.)

JAMIE: What are we going to do with Mom's things if we sell the house?

KAREN: I don't know. Give them away I guess.

JAMIE: *(Distressed.)* We can't. It's too soon.

KAREN: We have to. We have to sell the house. It's the only way we can pay for Dad.

JAMIE: I went to the farmers' market. Got lots of good greens. Got a ton of good stuff.   Lots of antioxidants. I've talked to him about it—drinking more smoothies and then working on his concentration. I think it's helping.

KAREN: He really drinks those?

JAMIE: Yeah. Well, not a whole one. I mean, he'll try a little. I usually finish it. He doesn't really like the taste.

(KAREN takes JAMIE'S hand.)

KAREN: It's hard to be alone. I wish we had a spare bedroom, but you'll just have to come over a lot for dinner. Ruby and Colin worship you.

JAMIE: They're great kids. *(Long pause.)* Karen, they don't have a *garden* there, where you're sending him. *(Pause.)* You know this house, this yard, this is Dad's world. If we make him leave, I can feel it, it's just going to take away all the rest of his spirit . . . and *he's going to die.* *(Tearing up.)* Do you know what I mean . . . ? Karen?

(KAREN'S looking away. She's teary now too. Motionless. Blackout.)

(Lights up on THE LIVING ROOM. ARTHUR is wandering between the kitchen counter and the couch, talking to himself, berating himself.)

ARTHUR: Vivian, Vivian, I don't like this. I get tired of all this . . . *(He straightens the pillows on the couch. Then starts to pace, agitated again.)* I *think* things—but it's not always clear. I would like to remember, because it would help. It would help me understand . . . *(He stops, holds up his hand, stares at his fingers. Obsessively he flexes his hand open and closed.)* You *dumbhead . . . dumbhead . . .*

(Blackout.)

(Lights up on THE BEDROOM. PETER, JAMIE and KAREN are standing at the bureau. PETER is holding Ruby's stuffed dog. KAREN opens the bottom drawer of the bureau.)

KAREN: *(To PETER.)* If you can't find something, this is where to look. It's what he does all day . . . *(She starts removing items from the drawer—a stapler, the two apples, a pepper grinder . . .)* You know he doesn't read anymore. He doesn't paint. He can only watch TV for about ten minutes, so he just kind of wanders around rearranging things . . . *(She takes out a tube of toothpaste wrapped in a washcloth.)* He likes to wrap things up and hide them. Mom found a quart of ice cream in here last fall. Remember that, Jamie?

49

JAMIE: What a mess.

(KAREN holds up a set of keys.)

KAREN: And *here* are your keys.

PETER: *(Taking the keys.)* This is the last place I would have looked.

JAMIE: Once he spent all morning stacking up books on the bathroom floor. That was a big day for him. He slept all afternoon on the couch.

PETER: *(With irritation.)* Now he's sleeping on the couch because he was wrapping up bananas till four AM. *(To Jamie.)* It's your turn in the living room tonight.

KAREN: Well, at least Dad's not paranoid. Debbie Bolson told me her grandmother would try to hide every time the doorbell rang because she thought they were coming to arrest her. We're lucky Dad's in a good mood most of the time.

PETER: *(Darkly.)* He won't be after Sunday.

KAREN: Do you think he'll even know what's going on? Do you really think we need to tell him?

JAMIE: I don't think we need to tell him. He was here the whole time. Deep down he *knows*. He just doesn't want to be reminded about it. *(Pause, quietly.)* It hurts too much.

PETER: I don't think he does *know*. Or if he did, he doesn't remember.

KAREN: *(To Peter.)* I took him to the hospital to visit her. I don't think I told you. It was before you flew in. *(Remembering)* It wasn't a good idea. He refused to get out of the car. I think maybe he knew.

PETER: I'm sorry, Karen. You've really had the worst of it.

KAREN: No, Mom had the worst of it . . . I really don't know how she did it these last few years. Especially after she got sick.

JAMIE: *(Pause, trying to keep it together.)* I miss her.

PETER: *(Caustic.)* Yeah, well maybe you should have been around a little more and helped her out with Dad.

JAMIE: *(Annoyed.)* You should talk. Too busy with your *big important job* product whatevering out there in Chicago to even come and visit. And when you do show up, you stay in a hotel. I live here, remember?

PETER: No, you don't *live* here. You eat here. You live at what's-her-name's house or you're at *Burning Man* or at some yoga place in the desert that Mom and Dad paid for.

JAMIE: You're so full of it. You have no clue. I told Karen I would take care of Dad. *(To Karen, creeping desperation)* Didn't I? He doesn't have to go. I can live here and watch him. You don't have to sell the house.

KAREN: Jamie, we've talked about it. It's a nice thought, that you want to do that. But honestly, I don't think you could handle it. I don't think any of us could handle it.

JAMIE: I have fun with Dad. We talk and hang out. I can get him to take his pills.

51

PETER: Are you kidding me? You watched him for five minutes and he wandered off. You don't want us to sell the house so that you won't have to go pay rent somewhere and live like an adult.

JAMIE: No, I just don't want to sell the house in case Dad hates it at that place where you're making him go. If I keep things up, if I mow the grass, if I weed the garden, it will all be here for him when he's ready to come back.

PETER: What are you, an idiot? I told you, he's *not* getting better.

JAMIE: Well, I think he *is* getting better. You know, doctors don't know everything. In fact, they don't know a lot of things.

PETER: Your brain is worse than his.

KAREN: *(To Jamie.)* I haven't gotten him to take off his socks in a week. His feet are starting to swell. He won't let me cut his toenails. Jamie, he needs help—and we just can't do it. *(Resolute.) We have to tell him.* One of us has to tell him about Mom and about . . . about what's going to happen.

PETER: *(Nodding.)* We owe him that much at least . . . *(Bursting, angry.)* Goddamit, I can barely look at him! When I think what this thing's doing to him. Dad taught for forty years. He was in the army. He published two books. He had a marriage that lasted forever. He was a success. He had respect. He *loved* respect . . . now he smells like a homeless guy. He won't brush his teeth. He cuts his own hair . . . he'd probably rather be dead than see himself like this. *(Completely serious.)* If I get Alzheimer's—put a bullet in my head.

JAMIE: Can I do it now?

PETER: Not *you*. Karen. I don't want *your* face to be the last thing I see.

JAMIE: You know, you think you'd want to die, but Dad's happy. He might not remember things—but he's happy. Maybe he has a different reality. Maybe he's living in a more truthful place. If Dad enjoys living, you can't just say he shouldn't be alive.

KAREN: That's true. Isn't happy *happy*? If in *his* mind he's okay, then isn't he okay?

PETER: *(To Karen)* Wait a minute. Do *you* think he's okay? Do you *really* think he's happy? I think he knows he can't remember. I think it makes him angry. I think it depresses him.

JAMIE: I don't think so, man. I don't think he even knows what he forgets. That's why he's at peace. That's why you shouldn't remind him about Mom. About tomorrow.

(PETER picks up the framed portrait of ARTHUR and VIVIAN from the top of the bureau, stares at it a long moment.)

PETER: I'll tell him this afternoon.

JAMIE: Peter, just don't do it. Please.

KAREN: Jamie, Dad may get upset but it's the right thing to do. We have to tell him what's happening . . . *he would want to know.* Dad's *old* self would want to know.

(They look at each other. Lights fade down on the bedroom.)

(Lights fade up. PETER and ARTHUR are sitting in THE GARDEN. ARTHUR is in the chair. PETER is on the bench. ARTHUR is gazing out intently at us.)

ARTHUR: *(Gesturing.)* I get awfully jealous of that green bush. See it against that gorgeous blue sky?

PETER: Maybe you should paint it.

ARTHUR: Yes, that would be nice. *(They sit for a long moment in silence.)*

PETER: *(Breaking the quiet.)* Dad, I have to tell you something. *(Pause, with difficulty.)* Your wife Vivian . . . our mother . . .

ARTHUR: *Vivian.*

PETER: She's gone away. She's not coming back. Ever. She died, Dad. She died last week. She had cancer for a long time and finally it was too much. I know you know this because you were here . . . you were here and you saw her every day until she got too sick, until she had to go back to the hospital . . . *(Pause.)* We're having her memorial service tomorrow. We thought we should tell you.

ARTHUR: *(Pause, still gazing out into the garden.)* I'm tremendously taken by those red flowers there. All I have to do is glance at those flowers and I feel excited, I feel intensely excited . . . and I don't need to have a rationale about what they do to me . . . but they do affect me, they do.

PETER: That's why you've seen Karen so much. And that's why I'm here now . . . but we can't be here forever. We have our own lives.

54

ARTHUR: I might have to close them down, because they're affecting me. Because they're so *alive*—so *present* . . .

PETER: We love you, but we think you need better care. We know you didn't like the nurse coming here. Monday we're going to bring you to a really nice place. It's like a big hotel. Then we'll talk about what things you want. Things to bring with you. All your favorite things. You'll have people around you all the time. I think you'll really like it.

> *(Pause.)*

ARTHUR: If I get up and walk into that house right now—it would be gone. *It would all be gone. (Long pause. Then Arthur leans forward, looks into Peter's eyes.)* I'm sorry, could you tell me your name again?

PETER: *(Pause.)* It's *Peter*, Dad . . . *(Softly.)* It's *Peter*.

> *(ARTHUR leans back in his chair, content now.)*

ARTHUR: Peter, it's really a pleasure to sit with you, here in the garden . . . *(A pause as he looks out over us.)* . . . it really is quite a pleasure.

> *(The two men sit, contemplate the garden. We hear the sounds of nature grow louder—of birds, of insects, of the wind rustling the trees. Then everything turns quiet and still as the light slowly fades to black.)*

END

RIDING THE WAVES

By

L.E. Grabowski-Cotton

57

INTRODUCTION—*Riding the Waves*

I am honored and grateful that my play was selected to be part of MemoryCare's Night of One Acts and included in this collection. I would like to thank MemoryCare and the actors and director who participated in MemoryCare's Night of One Acts. They were superb in their interpretations.

All of the plays in this collection center around the subject of dementia, a condition which causes memory loss, personality changes, and impaired reasoning. My connection to caregiving stems from several different places. When I was fifteen, my grandmother was hit by a van. She was walking to her job as a cafeteria lady at a local school when a driver backed up into her. As a result, her health, which had previously been excellent, began to fail. She was no longer able to live independently. She moved in with my family and my mom took care of her.

During this time, I experienced many of the joys that come with living with an elderly individual who has wisdom and life experience. But I also witnessed how much time and energy my mom had to sacrifice for her. This experience instigated my desire to write *Riding the Waves.*

I was also inspired to write *Riding the Waves* because of my own medical conditions. When I was twenty-five, I injured my back. I spent months on crutches and suffered from excruciating pain. Since that time, I have developed several other health related issues. As a result, I am drawn to people who are struggling with their health and well-being.

When I read the listing requesting plays that dealt with dementia, an image evolved within my mind. I saw a couple sitting by the beach, talking to each other. I thought that the sound of the waves could serve as memories, cues that would transport the main character and the audience back to the past. I wanted to show what it would be like to be inside the mind of someone with dementia. My objective was to relate her experience to audience members in a way which would open their eyes to the hardships that both the dementia sufferer and their caretakers face. The more I thought about it, the more inspired I became. But at the time, I was in too much physical pain to write.

The week before the play was due for MemoryCare's Competition, I felt stronger than I had felt in a long time. I decided that I would try to write this play. I had never written a one-act play so quickly and I wasn't sure it would be possible. Nevertheless, I couldn't resist trying. I devoted all of my time to writing and rewriting *Riding the Waves*. It was like I was being moved by a higher power, like God was speaking to me within the play, telling me what to write and how to write it. It was an incredible experience. A few months later, I transformed this one-act play into a full-length play, and that experience was equally profound.

I cannot predict if *Riding the Waves* will change anyone's perspective on dementia, but I know it changed me. It made me cognizant, insightful, and compassionate. I am so thankful that I was able to write it.

—L.E. Grabowski-Cotton

L.E. Grabowski-Cotton is a published writer, screenwriter, playwright, and professional writing coach. She holds an M.F.A. in Playwriting and Screenwriting from Florida State University, an M.A. in English Literature and a B.A. in Communication from George Mason University. She taught English Composition at The University of Memphis, Crichton College, and The New Bilingual Institute of George Mason University.

Each of her five full-length screenplays won multiple awards including placing in the top 10% of the Nicholl Fellowship, Table Read My Screenplay Sundance Film Festival, 20/20 Screenwriting

Contest, Fresh Voices Original Screenplay Contest, Scriptoid's Writer's Challenge, WriteMovies International Screenwriting Contest, American Zoetrope Screenplay Contest, and more.

Her monologues and plays were published in *Young Women's Monologues from Contemporary Plays* and *The Best Ten Minute Play* series. They have been performed all over the nation and placed in numerous contests.

In terms of fiction writing, her short story *The Mourning Dove* won first place in Literal Latte's Fiction Writing Contest, her story *Autumn Spring Together* placed in Women on Writing's Fiction Contest, and her story *The Women Who Lived In Shoes* placed in The 100 Hundred Words or Fewer Fiction Contest.

L.E. is currently querying agents for representation regarding her middle grade novel. For more information about her writing, please visit her website at LEGrabowskiCotton.Com. For more information about her coaching, please visit LauraWritingCoach.Com.

RIDING THE WAVES

By L.E. Grabowski-Cotton

SYNOPSIS

Riding the Waves tells the story of ISABEL EPSTEIN, a woman suffering from Alzheimer's disease, and the struggles her son and daughter experience as a result.

The inspiration for this play was the idea that the ocean could serve as a metaphor for the coming and going of memories. The waves interweave both ISABEL's past and present so that the audience experiences the plight of an individual with Alzheimer's.

CHARACTERS

ISABEL EPSTEIN—Early 60s. Glamorous, intelligent, and intuitive. Her Alzheimer's disease controls her mind, but it does not control her heart.

DAVID EPSTEIN, SR, otherwise known as HUSBAND DAVID— ISABEL's husband. Early 30s. A workaholic with a quirky sense of humor. He is alive only in ISABEL's mind, in the past.

DAVID EPSTEIN, JR, otherwise known as SON DAVID— ISABEL's son. Early 30s. Good-natured and compassionate. He also inherited his father's unique sense of humor. Throughout the play, he uses his comedic timing to lighten the heaviness of the mood.

NOTE: The same actor plays HUSBAND DAVID and SON DAVID. This is an intentional choice meant to disorient the audience so that it can achieve a deeper empathy for ISABEL's mental state.

SON DAVID wears a baseball cap; HUSBAND DAVID does not. When the actor becomes HUSBAND DAVID, he removes his baseball cap. When he becomes SON DAVID, he puts on his baseball cap. These actions are indicated within the play, but their importance is worth noting.

ELLY EPSTEIN—40s. ISABEL's daughter. A beautiful woman accustomed to getting her way. She loves her mother, but she doesn't understand her.

SETTING

Strive for simplicity. Two beach chairs with a large umbrella. Long beach towels are strewn over the chairs. One of the towels says, "Sunscreen is for Wimps" on it, but this isn't evident until later.

PLAYWRIGHT'S NOTE

This is a very visual play. Sounds and lights play a significant role in evoking the past and differentiating it from the present. The sounds of the ocean designate Isabel's past. The sound of the trees rustling in the breeze designate Isabel's present.

RIDING THE WAVES

A hazy morning at the beach. Waves crash, seagulls squawk, and children giggle.

(ISABEL, 60s, glamorous and intelligent, sits in a beach chair underneath an umbrella. She wears a dress over a stylish fifties-style bathing suit. She doesn't wear shoes. Next to ISABEL, engrossed in his newspaper, is HUSBAND DAVID. He wears a tee-shirt, shorts and flip-flops. There is a surreal quality to the day, as if it is someone's memory.)

ISABEL: *(Staring straight ahead at the ocean.)* She's in too deep.
(HUSBAND DAVID doesn't look up from his paper.)

HUSBAND DAVID: She's standing on the shore.

ISABEL: But she's close to the tide. And we don't know what could be in that water.

(HUSBAND DAVID turns the page of his paper.)

HUSBAND DAVID: Yeah, there's probably man-eating snails. Or blood sucking dolphins. Or maybe—*(Pauses and lowers his voice to an ominous whisper.)*—the Loch Ness Monster.

ISABEL: Ha ha. *(Shakes her head.)* I'd call to her, but she wouldn't listen to me. She prefers you. Because you spoil her.

HUSBAND DAVID: I don't spoil her. *(Playful.)* I just give her what she wants whenever she wants it.

ISABEL: You're ruining her is what you're doing. Last week she told me that she wished I would disappear. And all because I told her she couldn't eat ice cream for dinner.

HUSBAND DAVID: But she can have it for lunch?

ISABEL: *(She sighs.)* I went into the laundry room to do some ironing and when I came back upstairs, I found her in the kitchen. Gooey white cream was smeared all over her face, all over the cabinets, the floor, everything! It took over almost an hour just to clean everything up. And all that time, she just kept calling for you.

HUSBAND DAVID: That's funny. I didn't receive any calls.

ISABEL: Please, David. Try to listen. I do everything for her, but it doesn't matter. She only cares for you. You're her knight. Her knight in shining armor. *(Sadly.)* And what bothers me most of all is that you don't even realize how special you are. You give her whatever she wants, but that's not what she really needs. *(Beat.)* David? Are you listening to me? David?

> *(HUSBAND DAVID doesn't answer. The lighting grows harsher, more pronounced and less surreal. The sounds of the ocean fade away. A moment of silence. Then we hear the gentle sound of leaves rustling in the trees. DAVID puts down his newspaper. He takes a baseball cap out of his back pocket and puts it on. He is no longer Isabel's husband, but rather her SON DAVID. He's an attractive, kind-hearted man in his 30s.)*

SON DAVID: Yes, I'm listening.

ISABEL: *(Gazing at him in surprise.)* What?

SON DAVID: You were saying something about knights, right?

ISABEL: No, no. I was talking about Elly.

SON DAVID: Elly? Do you miss Elly?

ISABEL: *(Forehead wrinkling in confusion.)* What do you mean, miss her? Did she go away?

SON DAVID: She went to the beach, remember? Last Tuesday? But she's coming back today.

ISABEL: *(Trying to remember.)* Was she in the ocean? Was she swimming?

SON DAVID: I don't know. Probably.

ISABEL: *(Eyes widening.)* Did you tell her to come back?

SON DAVID: No, but she called a while ago. She'll be here any minute. She said she was looking forward to seeing you.

ISABEL: *(Shaking her head.)* That doesn't sound like Elly.

SON DAVID: You're right. Let me try again. How's this? *(Imitating ELLY's voice.)* I can't wait to see Mom.

(ISABEL laughs, then shakes her head.)

ISABEL: Elly was out playing. She was out having a grand time.

(ELLY enters. She's a beautiful woman in her forties and she knows it. She moves with an air of someone accustomed to getting her way. She wears a long red dress and a floppy white hat.)

SON DAVID: Elly!

(SON DAVID stands up and embraces ELLY.)

ELLY: Hi, David. Hi, Mom.

(ELLY leans over and hugs ISABEL.)

65

ISABEL: Not too tight. This is new. *(Proudly.)* David bought it for me.

ELLY: You bought her a dress?

SON DAVID: Not that I remember.

ELLY: Sometimes I think you're the one with Alzheimer's.

ISABEL: He just doesn't want to make you feel bad. Because he didn't get you anything.

(ELLY looks down at ISABEL and frowns.)

ELLY: You look red, Mom.

ISABEL: Well, you look green, Elly. *(Giggles)* Green with envy.

ELLY: *(To SON DAVID.)* Is she wearing sunscreen? Mom, are you wearing sunscreen?

(ISABEL tosses her head back in defiance.)

ISABEL: Sunscreen is for wimps.

ELLY: For wimps? David, where is she getting this from?

(SON DAVID picks up a beach towel. It reads "Sunscreen is for Wimps." He shows it to ELLY, then tosses it aside.)

SON DAVID: *(Feigning innocence.)* I have no idea.

ELLY: It's not funny, David. Look at this. *(Leaning over, she pulls ISABEL's strap, revealing ISABEL's scorched skin. ISABEL moves away from her, annoyed.)* You see how pink she is? This is why I told you not to let her outside. *(Looks around.)* Why are you out here anyway?

66

SON DAVID: She woke me up this morning. She said she wanted to see the sun rise. And then, all of the sudden she was in the closet, scrambling around for the old beach chairs.

ISABEL: I didn't want David to sit in the sand.

ELLY: The sand? What sand?

(SON DAVID shrugs and smiles. He sits back down in his chair.)

SON DAVID: The sand we're not sitting in?

ELLY: Well, thanks for taking care of her. I'm sure it wasn't easy.

ISABEL: Hmf. I could say the same thing about you.

ELLY: Sorry, Mom. I didn't mean it like that.

(ISABEL pats DAVID on the shoulder.)

ISABEL: David and I got along just fine. Didn't we, David?

SON DAVID: *(Nodding.)* Except for that big argument we had about the sailboat you bought.

ELLY: *(Alarmed.)* She bought a sailboat?!

ISABEL: Of course not. *(Beat.)* I bought a yacht.

(ELLY nearly passes out. She grabs hold of one the chairs to steady her body.)

ELLY: Oh my god.

SON DAVID: We're kidding.

ISABEL: *(Laughing.)* We sure fooled her, didn't we, David?

SON DAVID: Sure did.

ELLY: That wasn't funny. *(To SON DAVID.)* You really shouldn't say things like that. She's apt to believe you.

SON DAVID: Her? Or you?

ELLY: Shush. *(Leans over her mother's chair.)* Are you ready to go, Mom? Do you have your stuff packed? Do you need us to carry it down?

ISABEL: No, no, and no.

ELLY: What?

SON DAVID: *(Joking.)* I'm not sure, but I think she said no.

ELLY: This isn't funny, David. *(Extends her hand to ISABEL.)* Come on, Mom. It's time to go home now.

ISABEL: I'd rather stay here.

ELLY: You can't.

ISABEL: Why not?

ELLY: Because you don't live here.

ISABEL: But I could. I've always wanted a beach house.

SON DAVID: Good luck finding one here in Brooklyn.

ELLY: *(To SON DAVID.)* I knew this would happen. I knew the moment I left her, I'd return to trouble.

(ISABEL crosses her arms against her chest and glares at ELLY.)

ISABEL: Then maybe you should just leave again.

ELLY: Great. Now what am I supposed to do? Drag her out of here?

SON DAVID: Maybe I should talk to her. *(Beat.)* Why don't you go make her some tea or something?

ISABEL: I'd prefer a cocktail. Something light and breezy. What do you want, David?

SON DAVID: I'll have the same. But make mine a double, with extra breezy.

ELLY: Ha ha.

(ELLY disappears into the house.)

ISABEL: *(Shaking her head.)* She's not a very good waitress, is she? These beachside servers are never good. Yesterday I ordered a fruit cup, and do you know what I got? A spinach salad. There wasn't a single piece of fruit in it! Not even a tomato!

(SON DAVID takes ISABEL's hand.)

SON DAVID: Listen, I really enjoyed having you here, but you need to go with Elly now. You live with Elly. In Elly's house.

(Silence. Then ISABEL laughs and withdraws her hand.)

ISABEL: David, you're talking nonsense. Imagine Elly owning a house! Next you'll be saying that Elly drives a car!

SON DAVID: Elly does drive a car.

ISABEL: *(Laughs again.)* You really are funny today. She wouldn't even be able to see over the wheel! *(The sounds of the ocean return—the waves, the seagulls, etc. SON DAVID becomes HUSBAND DAVID. He takes off his baseball cap, picks up his newspaper, and resumes reading.)* But you do have a point. Elly is growing up fast. *(She sighs)* Really fast. Soon enough she *will* own a house and she will drive a car. And I'm afraid . . . I'm afraid you're missing it. You walk around with that paper over your eyes like it's a shield.

HUSBAND DAVID: I need to follow the stocks, Isabel.

ISABEL: The stocks, the stocks, that's all I ever hear about. One goes up, another goes down. You're riding the waves; that's what you're doing. And where is it getting you?

HUSBAND DAVID: That's easy. *(Holding his paper with one hand, he motions around with his other hand.)* To the beach.

ISABEL: You take one vacation a year. And yet you travel constantly. *(Beat.)* Where do you go, David?

HUSBAND DAVID: Oh, come on, Isabel. You know where I go.

ISABEL: I know some women wouldn't care. They'd find other ways to entertain themselves. They would shop or drink or go to potlucks. But I didn't marry you to go to a potluck, David.

HUSBAND DAVID: So why are you always making potato salad?

ISABEL: I married you so that we could spend our life together. I wanted us to take lavish trips to exotic locations. I wanted us to hold each other on freezing nights when it was snowing outside and there

70

was nothing to eat except for marshmallows. And most of all, I wanted us to be a family.

HUSBAND DAVID: The first idea is too expensive. The second is too sticky.

(Awkward silence.)

ISABEL: What about the third idea?

HUSBAND DAVID: We're already a family, Isabel.

(ISABEL shakes her head.)

ISABEL: Elly and I hardly see you. All you care about is money. Money all day, money all night. And how much do we really need? How much until we have enough? And when we have enough, how much more?

(HUSBAND DAVID turns the page of his paper.)

HUSBAND DAVID: Ask me that again when we have enough.

ISABEL: *(Shaking her head.)* All these jokes, all these quick retorts to everything I say. *(Raising her voice.)* You don't care about me at all, do you? Do you, David? Answer me, David!

(The lighting grows harsher, more pronounced and less surreal. The sounds of the ocean fade away. A moment of silence. Then we hear the gentle sound of leaves rustling in the trees. HUSBAND DAVID becomes SON DAVID. He puts down his newspaper and puts on his baseball cap.)

SON DAVID: Of course I care about you.

71

ISABEL: You don't! You hate me!

(She bursts into tears. ELLY enters. She carries a tray with two cups of steaming tea on it.)

ELLY: Is everything okay?

(She puts the tray down on DAVID's beach chair.)

SON DAVID: Yeah. Mom is just screaming her head off.

ELLY: *(Shaking her head.)* Welcome to my world.

(ISABEL refuses to look at ELLY.)

SON DAVID: She was fine up until you came back.

ELLY: So it's my fault now?

SON DAVID: That's not what I'm saying.

ISABEL: I don't want her here. Not now. Not for this.

SON DAVID: Elly, maybe you should come back in a few minutes.

ELLY: Dr. Worthington said we shouldn't give in to her.

ISABEL: *(Shutting her eyes.)* Tell her, David! Tell her to go away!

SON DAVID: Please, Elly.

ELLY: *(Sighing.)* Fine. Fifteen more minutes. We have to take the train back, you know, and I don't want to be riding on it at midnight.

(ELLY goes back inside.)

ISABEL: Is she gone?

SON DAVID: The coast appears to be clear.

(The sounds of the ocean return—the waves, the seagulls, etc. SON DAVID becomes HUSBAND DAVID. He takes off his baseball cap and picks up his newspaper.)

ISABEL: I didn't want her to hear us. It's not good for a little girl to hear her parents fight.

HUSBAND DAVID: So we're fighting now?

ISABEL: I know you're stressed about money. But I thought . . . I thought things were getting better for us.

HUSBAND DAVID: *(Sorrowful.)* They're not. We shouldn't even be here right now.

ISABEL: *(With envy.)* But Elly begged you, right? And you can never say no to her.

HUSBAND DAVID: You both begged me.

(ISABEL stands up. She gazes out at the water.)

ISABEL: I just wanted us to get away for a while. I thought that maybe if I could take you away, you'd forget all about . . . All about . .
.

HUSBAND DAVID: All about what?

(ISABEL turns around and looks HUSBAND DAVID straight in the eyes.)

ISABEL: *(Quietly, almost whispering.)* Her.

HUSBAND DAVID: What are you talking about?

73

ISABEL: I found part of a letter, David. I didn't mean to find it. But I was cleaning one day, and you left it out. You said not to worry, that you would take care of her. That everything would be fine. *(With quiet control.)* Who is she?

HUSBAND DAVID: *(Getting upset.)* You were going through my things?

ISABEL: I was just trying to clean up for you.

HUSBAND DAVID: Well, you ended up making more of a mess.

(Silence.)

ISABEL: Are you in love with her?

HUSBAND DAVID: It's not like that.

ISABEL: Then what is it like, David? Is it sex?

HUSBAND DAVID: *(Annoyed.)* No.

ISABEL: Then what?

HUSBAND DAVID: I can't tell you.

ISABEL: Why not?

HUSBAND DAVID: Because you wouldn't understand.

ISABEL: Please, David. Please tell me.

HUSBAND DAVID: *(Shaking his head.)* You'd tell me to stop helping her.

(Silence. ISABEL collapses into her chair, as if struck by lightning.)

ISABEL: *(Realizing what he is saying.)* Oh my god. That's where all the money's been going, hasn't it?

HUSBAND DAVID: *(Quietly.)* She needs it more than we do.

ISABEL: How can you say that? When I'm your wife? When we have a child?

HUSBAND DAVID: Because it's true!

ISABEL: Well then, you should be with her. Wouldn't that make everything easier? Leave Elly and me and go and live with her?

> *(The lighting grows harsher, more pronounced and less surreal. The sounds of the ocean fade away. A moment of silence. Then we hear the gentle sound of leaves rustling in the trees. HUSBAND DAVID becomes SON DAVID. He puts down his newspaper and puts on his baseball cap.)*

SON DAVID: No, you're confused. You're leaving me.

ISABEL: I would never leave you, David.

SON DAVID: *(Tenderly.)* It's only temporary. I'll visit you in a few weeks. And you'll be busy. You have your water aerobics, your Bingo, your ballroom dancing.

ISABEL: I've never danced a day in my life.

SON DAVID: Of course you have. Elly says you're really good.

ISABEL: *(Scornfully.)* She's telling stories.

SON DAVID: Let's see.

75

ISABEL: Let's see what?

(SON DAVID goes into the house. A moment later, he emerges, carrying a cd player and two cds.)

SON DAVID: Waltz or foxtrot?

ISABEL: I told you. I don't dance.

SON DAVID: A waltz it is.

(SON DAVID puts one of the cds into the player. It begins to play. SON DAVID takes ISABEL's hand and leads her through a waltz. At first, he is dragging her, but then she follows. It's clear she knows how to dance. After a few moments, ISABEL speaks.)

ISABEL: This is nice. Your father didn't dance, you know.

SON DAVID: No?

ISABEL: He used to say he had two right feet.

SON DAVID: You mean two left ones?

ISABEL: No. Two right ones. Because—*(Imitating HUSBAND DAVID's voice.)*—"If you have two right feet, neither one can be wrong." *(Laughs.)* He had a sense of humor. It was impossible to stay angry with him.

SON DAVID: *(Joking.)* He was a serious guy then, huh?

ISABEL: *(Misunderstanding.)* What? Oh, no. David was . . . He was a lot like you.

SON DAVID: *(Nodding.)* You get us confused sometimes.

ISABEL: *(Alarmed.)* Do I?

SON DAVID: Only sometimes.

ISABEL: I should never have named you after him.

SON DAVID: Nah. He should never have been named after me.

(ISABEL smiles. A moment passes. Then suddenly, without warning, ISABEL pulls away from SON DAVID.)

ISABEL: What am I doing? What are we doing?

SON DAVID: We were dancing. Remember?

(He makes a few funny dance moves.)

ISABEL: *(Agitated.)* No, no. We were sitting down. I was telling you how I found the letter and you were saying . . . You were saying. . . David, what were you saying?!

(The sounds of the ocean return—the waves, the seagulls, etc. ISABEL and DAVID sit back down on the beach chairs. SON DAVID becomes HUSBAND DAVID. He takes off his baseball cap and picks up his newspaper.)

HUSBAND DAVID: You have to trust me, Isabel. I'm doing the right thing.

ISABEL: Then why can't you tell me who she is?

HUSBAND DAVID: I told you why!

(Silence.)

ISABEL: I can't live like this, David.

HUSBAND DAVID: *(Joking.)* That's good, because we can't afford it.

ISABEL: I'm serious.

HUSBAND DAVID: *(Still joking.)* So am I. *(He takes a sip of tea.)* We're going to have to take out a second mortgage just to pay for these drinks.

>*(ISABEL can't help but smile.)*

ISABEL: *(Frustrated.)* You always do that. Even when I'm really upset you always make me smile.

HUSBAND DAVID: Look, Isabel. We're going to be okay. We've been okay this long, we'll be okay a little longer. We just can't be extravagant that's all.

>*(Silence.)*

ISABEL: When we get home, I'm taking Elly and we're leaving.

HUSBAND DAVID: You don't mean that, Isabel.

ISABEL: I do. This isn't right.

HUSBAND DAVID: It is. You have to trust me on this.

ISABEL: No. You shouldn't have to work so hard. *(Becoming upset again.)* Especially not for another woman!

HUSBAND DAVID: I'm not doing it for her.

ISABEL: Then who are you doing it for? *(Silence.)* Answer me, David. Please. Please just answer me.

(HUSBAND DAVID doesn't answer. The lighting grows harsher, more pronounced and less surreal. The sounds of the ocean fade away. A moment of silence. Then we hear the gentle sound of leaves rustling in the trees. HUSBAND DAVID becomes SON DAVID. He puts down his newspaper and puts on his baseball cap.)

SON DAVID: I'm doing it for you. *(Beat.)* You're better off with Elly. She knows how to take care of you.

(ELLY reenters, lugging ISABEL's suitcase.)

ELLY: I brought down her stuff.

(SON DAVID stands up and takes the suitcase from ELLY.)

ISABEL: Where did you meet her?

(SON DAVID puts the suitcase down and looks at ISABEL.)

SON DAVID: Who?

ELLY: Her!

SON DAVID: *(To ELLY.)* She's not herself right now.

ELLY: But she was before?

SON DAVID: She was here for a second. When we were dancing. But now she's gone again.

ISABEL: *(To SON DAVID.)* At least tell me her name. Surely you can tell me her name!

ELLY: My name is Elly, Mom. Elly. I'm your daughter, remember? *(To SON DAVID.)* This is my fault. I took her out of her home. I took her away from her nurse. And for what? A few days at the beach?

SON DAVID: You deserved a break.

ISABEL: But we couldn't afford a break. You said so yourself.

ELLY: *(Shaking her head.)* She's suffering now because of it. Because of me.

ISABEL: *(Holding back tears.)* This has nothing to do with you, Elly. Run along now, and play with your toys. Build a sandcastle.

ELLY: A sandcastle? *(She wrings her hands through her hair.)* Do you think she's doing this on purpose? Do you think she's trying to torment me for leaving her?

SON DAVID: No. No, I think she really thinks she's at the beach.

ISABEL: *(Still holding back tears.)* Would you tell her to go, David? She listens to you better than me.

SON DAVID: I think she's asking for more time.

ELLY: More time? She's already been with you for a week.

SON DAVID: Five more minutes.

ELLY: Fine. But then that's it. I'll carry her out of here if I have to.

(ELLY goes back into the house. The sounds of the ocean return—the waves, the seagulls, etc. SON DAVID becomes HUSBAND DAVID. He sits back down. He takes off his baseball cap and picks up his newspaper.)

HUSBAND DAVID: I'm doing it for you.

ISABEL: For me? You're taking care of some stranger for me.

HUSBAND DAVID: She's not a stranger. *(Beat.)* She's your mother.

ISABEL: What? What are you talking about?

(HUSBAND DAVID stands up. He walks out and gazes out at the sea. Then he turns around and looks at ISABEL.)

HUSBAND DAVID: Do you remember last Christmas, when Milo came to see us?

ISABEL: Milo? You mean my brother, Milo?

HUSBAND DAVID: He didn't just come to visit.

ISABEL: What do you mean?

HUSBAND DAVID: He came to ask for help. He told me that your mother was sick. Sick in a way that the doctors didn't understand. That no one understood. She was saying things, doing things that didn't make sense. One moment, she'd be fine. She'd be behaving just as she always had, sculpting her pots or painting her pictures. The next moment, she'd become agitated, confused about who she was and what she was doing.

ISABEL: That doesn't sound like my mother.

HUSBAND DAVID: She couldn't take care of herself. She'd wander outside and forget where she was going. She'd stare at Milo and ask him who he was. She didn't know what time it was, or what day, or even what year. It was like she was losing her mind.

81

ISABEL: So Milo came and asked you for money for her? And you gave it to him without even consulting me?

HUSBAND DAVID: No. *(Beat.)* I went to see her first.

ISABEL: You? The Jewish boy from the Bronx? You went to see my Upper East Side mother?

HUSBAND DAVID: She doesn't live on the Upper East Side anymore, Isabel. She lives in Cincinnati.

ISABEL: Cincinnati? *(Makes a face.)* No wonder she's losing her mind.

HUSBAND DAVID: Milo thought it would be best if she lived near him.

ISABEL: I can't believe he didn't tell me. I can't believe *you* didn't tell me.

HUSBAND DAVID: We wanted to tell you. But you hadn't spoken in years. Milo was afraid you were still mad at her.

ISABEL: I *was* still mad at her! I invited her to our wedding. She refused to come. She said that I'd go straight to hell if I married you. *(Shakes her head.)* And all because you weren't Catholic.

HUSBAND DAVID: Really? *(Joking.)* And all this time, I thought it was because I have freckles.

ISABEL: It's the same thing. She hated anyone who wasn't exactly like her. Black people, Chinese people, Spanish people. Anyone who looked different, who acted different. Why would I want to be around someone like that?

HUSBAND DAVID: *(Quietly)* Because she's your mother.

ISABEL: *(Shaking her head.)* You don't know. I didn't want to upset you, to make you feel like it was your fault. But after we married, she locked me out of her life. I called her. I tried to talk to her. But every time I did, she would just hang up the phone.

HUSBAND DAVID: You should have told me.

ISABEL: It's not a big deal. *(Beat.)* So that letter . . . That letter was to . . . *(Confused.)* My mother?

HUSBAND DAVID: Yes. I write to her. You know, to check in on her, to see how she's doing. She thinks I'm her secret admirer. I know it's strange, but the doctors say it's good for her. They say it makes her happy.

> *(ISABEL stares at him. She stands up and paces.)*

ISABEL: So all this time, all this time, you've been cheating on me with my mother?

HUSBAND DAVID: Oh, come on. She's eighty-two, Isabel.

ISABEL: I don't mean cheating in the physical sense. I mean, lying. Pretending.

HUSBAND DAVID: What else could I do? Your brother asked for my help. I helped him. Your mother needed my help. I helped her. That's what families do.

ISABEL: I would have helped her!

HUSBAND DAVID: Well, Milo didn't want to take the chance of you saying no. And when I saw her, Isabel, when I saw her in that

83

home, I couldn't take the chance of you saying no. She's seeing a specialist now. She takes medication. I don't know if it will help her or not, but at least it's something.

(Silence.)

ISABEL: But what about you? You're working so hard and for what? For my mother? A woman who never even liked you?

HUSBAND DAVID: You see? This is why I never told you.

ISABEL: I just don't want you to miss out!

HUSBAND DAVID: Miss out on what?

ISABEL: On your life! On our life!

(HUSBAND DAVID puts his arms around ISABEL, embracing her.)

HUSBAND DAVID: This is our life, Isabel. Our daughter, that beautiful little girl playing over there, she is our life. *(Beat.)* Everything I did, I did for you. I love you, Isabel. I'll always love you.

(The lighting grows harsher, more pronounced and less surreal. The sounds of the ocean fade away. A moment of silence. Then we hear the gentle sound of leaves rustling in the trees. ISABEL and DAVID sit back down in the beach chairs. HUSBAND DAVID becomes SON DAVID. He puts on his baseball cap.)

ISABEL: I was too hard on him. I didn't understand.

SON DAVID: Who?

ISABEL: Your father. He was more giving than me. More generous.

84

SON DAVID: No. You were the one who raised us. We barely saw Dad.

ISABEL: *(Crying.)* He gave us everything. Everything he had. And what did I give him?

SON DAVID: Two kids? A family?

ISABEL: That's not enough! *(Stands up and paces.)* I kept nagging him. Even after that day at the beach. I asked him how much money he was sending her, what he said in his letters, why he had to write so many. And when he went to see her, I didn't go. My own mother. I hated her. I hated her because I felt like she was taking him away from me.

(SON DAVID stands up. He places his hand on ISABEL's shoulder.)

SON DAVID: It's okay. It's in the past.

ISABEL: It's not. It's still happening. Don't you see? Don't you understand?

SON DAVID: No. No, it's over now.

ISABEL: It isn't. Because I never told you.

SON DAVID: Told me what?

ISABEL: That I'm sorry. Oh, David. I'm so sorry. Can you ever forgive me?

(Silence. Then the sound of the waves returns. But we are still in the present.)

SON DAVID: *(Deciding to play along.)* Yes. Yes, of course, I forgive you.

(ISABEL embraces SON DAVID, throwing her arms around him.)

ISABEL: Thank you.

(The sound of the waves fades away. ELLY returns.)

ELLY: Okay. It's been more than five minutes. Time to go.

SON DAVID: *(To ISABEL)* Are you ready?

ISABEL: What? Oh, yes. Yes, of course. I've been ready. I can't lie on the beach forever, you know. I'll get burned.

ELLY: You weren't at the beach, Mom. I was at the beach.

ISABEL: We were all at the beach, Elly. *(ISABEL takes SON DAVID's hand, then ELLY's hand. She stands between them, gazing out at something in the distance. The lighting becomes hazy. The sound of the waves return.)* You, me, your father. *(Looks at SON DAVID and smiles.)* And little David, I didn't even know about you yet, but you were there too. We were all together. It was a lovely day. *(Beat.)* I'll never forget it.

(Lights fade.)

END

DISCUSSION QUESTIONS

Steering Into the Skid by Deborah Ann Percy and Arnold Johnston

Discussion Questions

1) Although the progressive loss of functional abilities would be slower for the average person with Alzheimer's disease, the playwrights have utilized one of the most challenging issues, driving, to dramatize the loss of independence that comes with dementia. At the beginning of the play when Tim and Amanda are driving home from their New Year's Eve party, Tim almost misses a turn and Amanda excuses it by stating he's just upset to have left before he was ready. Is it common for spouses to excuse or rationalize the memory lapses of loved ones early in dementia?

2) Over the next few months there are subtle changes: confusion over the right routes when driving and difficulty embracing new technology (GPS, remote controls).

   a) Do cognitively normal older people often struggle in the same areas?
   b) Would you consider Tim's difficulties in these areas suggestive of a serious problem? Why or why not?

3) What are some of the more significant memory problems displayed by Tim in the late spring through early summer?

4) Individuals with cognitive impairment often lack insight to the degree that it impacts their daily function.

   a) How insightful do you think Tim is about his loss of memory function?
   b) How might lack of insight impact the caregiver relationship?

5) Tim expresses some paranoia regarding Amanda's desire to speak to their son when he is "out of earshot". Why do families feel they cannot always include the person with dementia in their conversations?

6) Anything less than complete honesty is very challenging for spousal caregivers, yet as the dementia progresses, attempts at full transparency often lead to agitation and distress for the person with dementia.

   a) How does Amanda try to soften the transition regarding taking over driving and hiring an in-home companion when she is working?
   b) What safety issues might arise if she did not?

7) What strengths do you see in this couple's relationship that will help them along the difficult road ahead?

In the Garden by Matthew Widman

Discussion Questions

1) The playwright describes Arthur Monsetin as a "gentleman who manages to maintain his underlying dignity despite his disease". Maintaining dignity for a loved one is an extremely important issue for families affected by Alzheimer's disease or any type of dementia.

   a) What do you think families mean by this phrase ("maintaining dignity")?
   b) How was Arthur Monsetin's dignity threatened?

2) Jamie and Peter's personalities are distinctly different. Jamie's more relaxed approach to their father's dementia is judged as irresponsible by his brother.

   a) What concerns are raised?
   b) What possible benefits might there be from such a perspective?

3) Initially Karen and Peter do not choose to remind their father that her mother, Vivian, has recently passed away. Is that a constructive approach? Why or why not?

4) Jamie felt justified to take some money from his dad's wallet and mother's purse.

   a) How did that make you feel?
   b) Did your discomfort resolve when he asked his dad if it was OK to borrow it?
   c) Jamie offered to be his father's caregiver; why didn't Peter and Karen take him up on it?

5) Karen lists a number of stresses that have arisen with her parent's situation: time away from her husband and children, her daughter's fear of her grandfather's dementia-related behaviors, difficulty getting time off work for caregiving duties, and her father mistaking her for her mother.

   a) Which of these are unique to caregiving for someone with dementia?
   b) What are some other caregiving stresses that are unique to dementia?

6) Arthur exhibits abrupt mood shifts and changes in personality which create challenges for his children. Anger, hostility, paranoia, and stubbornness can be common in dementia. Agitated behaviors can be triggered by well-meaning caregivers and similarly soothed by trained responses. What triggers can be identified and where do the children respond in ways that defuse agitated behaviors?

7) Jamie expresses great fear that moving their father will crush his spirit and hasten his death.

   a) Could a move be avoided?
   b) What are the potentially positive aspects of facility care for someone with dementia?

8) On several occasions in the play Arthur refers to himself as a "dumbhead". Does he have insight to his condition during these times?

9) Arthur likes to spend his waking hours walking around "rearranging things". Why might that be a commonly observed behavior for people with dementia?

10) It appears that the Monsetin children had no idea how impaired their father was until after their mother's death.

   a) Is this a common scenario?
   b) Why do parents attempt to shield adult children from the reality of dementia?

11) Peter states he'd rather take a bullet to the head than have Alzheimer's but Jamie and Karen remind him that their father is happy. Would you agree that Alzheimer's is often more difficult for the family than for the person suffering the disease?

12) Despite his confusion, there are moments when Arthur does fulfill his role as a father. Where does that play out?

13) There is a valuable transition when caregivers "cross the bridge" to live in the person with dementia's world. When are there instances where this happens for the Monsetin children?

Riding the Waves, by L.E. Grabowski-Cotton

Discussion Questions

1) The playwright uses an ocean metaphor to help the audience experience the erosion of lines between present and past for a person with Alzheimer's disease. While clinically it is not usually this dramatic, caregivers often experience their own confusion when a loved one seems to shift in orientation from day to day or hour to hour.

   a) How does this concept impact you as the reader/viewer?
   b) What similar experiences have you had when engaged in relationship with a person with dementia?

2) The average age for onset of Alzheimer's disease is after 75 yet Isabel is afflicted in her early 60's. While less than 5% of persons with Alzheimer's disease have early onset disease (before age 65), how might it raise different issues than later onset dementia?

3) Elly, Isabel's daughter, casually states to her brother, "I think you're the one with Alzheimer's," in front of their mother. Many families work to protect a loved one from hearing that term.

   a) Why?
   b) Was Elly's comment insensitive?

4) David and Elly have different personalities and modes of interacting with their mother. Why does Isabel appear to prefer her son's company?

5) Elly seems stressed and burdened by David's carefree, "live in the moment" attitude. Often the primary caregiver carries

most of the workload. How can secondary caregivers provide more relief?

6) Delusions of infidelity are not uncommon for persons with dementia, even in the most stable long-term relationships. How does the structure of Isabel and David's marriage fuel her dementia-related paranoia that David does not care about her and had an affair?

7) Elly makes the statement, "Dr. Worthington says we shouldn't give into her," when Isabel is demanding her way. Is that sound advice?

8) Elly expresses fear and guilt that she is responsible for Isabel's increased confusion due to taking a week of respite while David cared for their mother. This is a common theme for caregivers yet they desperately need to have breaks.

   a) Is there a better solution for this dilemma?
   b) How would you comfort Elly?

9) In the midst of her guilt and concern, Elly also questions whether her mother is exhibiting difficult behavior intentionally to punish her.

   a) How would you answer?
   b) What might help improve Elly's perspective?

10) We learn that Isabel's mother also had Alzheimer's disease. Early onset Alzheimer's is likely to have a stronger genetic component than late onset Alzheimer's disease. How might this impact Elly and David?

INSTRUCTIONS FOR UTILIZING THESE PLAYS

The playwrights of these three one act plays have graciously granted MemoryCare the authority to grant other nonprofit organizations dedicated to dementia care a non-exclusive, royalty free license to perform the approved version of their plays, in whole or in part, at any educational, advocacy or fundraising event, provided that such nonprofit organization agrees that all profits raised from any such event will be applied to the care or support of persons affected by dementia. Any license granted by MemoryCare to a nonprofit organization dedicated to dementia care shall be granted on a single-use basis and the playwright shall be notified when MemoryCare grants a license for the performance of their work. In all printed, published and licensed performances of the approved work, whole or part, the playwright must be credited. If only part of the play is published, printed or performed, it must be acknowledged in the credits that the presented work is part of a longer work by the playwright. Any person or entity requesting to perform these plays that is not a non-profit organization dedicated to dementia care will be referred directly to the playwright.

For further information on utilizing these plays for educational, advocacy, or fundraising purposes, please contact MemoryCare. Contact information can be found at www.memorycare.org.

ACKNOWLEDGEMENTS

First and foremost, I extend my gratitude to the four playwrights who agreed to generously share their work in a format that will benefit so many. Whether their works are staged or read, they are rich with authenticity and instruction. The beautiful artwork gracing the cover of this anthology by Harry Widman is kindly provided from the collection of his son, playwright Matthew Widman. The process of selecting these three plays from over ninety submissions to the competition required many hands, including those who provide care day in and day out to persons with dementia. Author Tommy Hays, actress and former theatre manager Paige Poscy, and MemoryCare's director Dr. Virginia Templeton served as jurors who did the final selection of the plays that are included in this anthology, giving their valuable time to carefully read and rank the top submissions.

Blessings to the wonderful people of Grace Centre including Craig Lotz, Dusty McNabb Campbell, Dick and Saundra Cuyler, Lori and McCrae Hilliard, David Hudson, Ed Mathis, Chari Moss, Matt Moss, Catherine Zayatz and others who gave life to these plays and brought the audience to a fuller understanding of how dementia impacts families.

MemoryCare's Chad Conaty assisted with the promotion and logistics of the final production as well as the supervision of our army of volunteers who made the evening of one acts flawless. Dr. Laurel Coleman provided guidance and participated to make the award ceremony especially meaningful to the playwrights. I am indebted to Jessica Dement, Anne Gardner, Diane Gage and Sarah Morris for their technical help and editing assistance. My special thanks to Karen Gledhill and Ashley Hedgecock of Robinson Bradshaw & Hinson, P.A. for overseeing contractual matters for this work and general assistance to MemoryCare.

The work of MemoryCare would be impossible without the philanthropic support of over 45 foundations, churches, temples and other charitable entities that have provided funding through the years along with the generous financial and volunteer time commitments of many individuals. Their kind hands have encouraged us in innumerable, immeasurable ways to do this work and I am most grateful to all who have helped build this program and to all who seek to sustain its work long into the future.

And lastly to those who inspired and encouraged me personally along the way, my patients and their families, my colleagues at MemoryCare, and my family, especially my husband and greatest supporter, John—you deserve my heartfelt thanks for helping create this privileged place to practice medicine in a way that makes a profound difference in the lives that are touched.

— Margaret A. Noel, MD

CPSIA information can be obtained at www.ICGtesting.com
Printed in the USA
LVOW01s1618050615

441363LV00022B/1056/P